The Council

A Dialogue with
Catholic Traditionalism

The Council in Question

A Dialogue with Catholic Traditionalism

Moyra Doorly
Aidan Nichols, OP

Freedom **Publishing**
AUSTRALIA

GRACEWING

First published in 2011

Gracewing
2 Southern Avenue, Leominster
Herefordshire HR6 0QF
United Kingdom

Published in Australia
by
Freedom Publishing Pty Ltd
35 Whitehorse Road
Balwyn
Victoria 3103

ISBN 978 085244 765 9

Typeset by Action Publishing Technology Ltd,
Gloucester GL1 5SR

Printed in England by
The MPG Books Group, King's Lynn PE30 4LS

Contents

Foreword

Recently I have been reading Eamon Duffy's *Fires of Faith: Catholic England under Mary Tudor* (2009) which recounts the heroic efforts of Queen Mary and Cardinal Reginald Pole, Archbishop of Canterbury, to replant the Catholic Faith in England and how they nearly succeeded. One cause of anguish as I read of the changing circumstances in this struggle was the officially endorsed burning of Protestants, often simple-minded heroes who could not be dissuaded. Both sides, Catholic and Protestant, believed it just and sometimes necessary to eliminate their opponents. St Thomas More was responsible for a number of Protestant deaths.

All Christians today have radically different sensibilities from our sixteenth-century Christian brothers and sisters who were pro-burning. This is progress, a genuine and homogeneous doctrinal development which spells out better the consequences of the Gospel. Vatican II was correct to acknowledge the rights of persons not to be coerced by the State in their religious convictions.

Much more could be said about these facts, on human dignity, Christendom and the coercive powers of State and Church to remind us that learned dialogue has to be seen in wider theological and cultural perspectives. All Christians are nourished by the Scriptures and Catholics reverence the teachings of Popes and Councils, while the historical, political and public relations consequences of doctrinal and disciplinary developments have to be carefully considered – better than we have done recently.

The stimulating debate in this book is like a tennis match between Trent and Vatican II, between two players with strongly contrasting styles. Trent has a powerful and well-placed serve, the occasional devastating smash, and volleys efficiently at the net when she gets into position. Vatican II possesses only an ordinary serve, but plays a wide variety of strokes including topspin, and is fast and agile around the court. On some occasions Father Nichols had to work hard to keep the ball in play but he was regularly successful.

Without doubt the Catholic Church everywhere in the English-speaking world is now very different from the Church of the 1950s. The bigger changes came from outside pressures, e.g. the pill, and the consequent permissive revolution, the coarsening of standards in the new media, and hostile legislation. But many Catholic communities have been guilty also of self-harm, ignorantly encouraging the secularization of institutions. When the reforms of Vatican II were imposed, unexpected consequences followed, especially when leaders were naïve and optimistic, underestimating the virulence of hostile forces and overestimating Catholic vitality and influence. The crux of the discussion is whether this self-harm came from illegitimate appeals to 'the spirit of Vatican II' or can be sheeted home to doctrinal errors in the Council teachings.

We now have situations which are historically novel, indeed bizarre in a couple of opposite ways. Some still insist on calling themselves Catholic when they reject most of the Church's teaching on life, marriage and sexuality and regard the Pope and Bishops as hindrances (or irrelevant) to their modernizing projects. We had one priest in Australia who generated considerable publicity before he left his parish because he rejected the Judaeo-Christian concept of God as tribal and rejected the divinity of Christ who, he felt, might not have existed. For years he claimed to be Catholic.

On the other hand, with the Society of St Pius X we have devout believers who accept the Tradition but face resolutely

at the same time in different directions by separating themselves from the legitimate authority of Pope and the Council,
while also speaking as though they were more Catholic than
the Pope, prepared to 'write the creed with their own blood'.

I fear that the term 'official Church' increases the
confusion. For years I have refused to use it, because there is
no such thing as 'the official Church', especially if contrasted
with local 'spontaneous' communities. The one Catholic
Church, the Orthodox churches and other ecclesial communities all have officials, but that is a different matter.

This fascinating exchange is a significant contribution to
the official dialogue between Rome and Ecône but is of
wider significance in searching out the nature of genuine
continuity and development across the millennia in
doctrine, liturgy, and church law; and in devising pastoral
strategies for handing on the faith and for re-evangelization.

It is a lively reminder that none of us can take refuge in
fundamentalisms, and deserves to be read widely.

✠ George Cardinal Pell
Archbishop of Sydney

Feast of St Vincent de Paul
27 September 2010

The Making of a Debate:
A View from the Official Church

Thinking ahead to his coming Council (Vatican II, 1962-1965), Pope John XXIII described it as devoted to the 'enlightenment, edification, and joy of the entire Christian people'. At around the same time, the Archbishop of Milan, who would become, as Paul VI, the second (and last) pope of the Council, gave vent to his fear it would stir up a 'hornets' nest'. Both predictions were, up to a point, correct. The exchange of letters in this book bears witness to that.

What, we may ask, was the aim, initially, of the Second Vatican Council? The answer is not easy to give because John XXIII – whose personal brain-child it was – gave rather conflicting signals about the contents of his own mind. But we should not go far wrong if we included in our answer a trio of goals. They were: giving inspiration for the Church's witness to the contemporary world; providing an impetus to the reunion of Christians; recovering more fully some ancient features of the Tradition (a more rounded reading of the Bible, knowledge of the Fathers, and early Christian spirituality – including liturgical spirituality – would have figured among the 'features' concerned). It is likely that the Pope expected the Council, to some degree, to define itself. When, by its documents, it did so, it became apparent that the first and the third of the goals just suggested, soon to be dubbed, in a borrowing from, respectively, Italian – *aggiornamento* or 'bringing up to date' – and French – *ressourcement* or 'going back to the sources' – did indeed describe what the Council's overall presentation of Catholicism was meant to achieve.

At the same time, the second goal, ecumenism, though chiefly confined to one document in particular, became in popular perception, at any rate in Western countries, the Second Vatican Council's most distinctive mark. I should add, somewhat as a parenthesis, that Pope John's decision to call the Council the Second Council *of the Vatican* has also been taken to imply that he expected the assembly of bishops to complete the unfinished work of the (abruptly interrupted) First Vatican Council (1869-1870) by providing a fuller account of the nature of the Church – and not least of the position of the episcopate vis-à-vis the Papacy.

In conformity to Pope John's (probable) expectation, the Conciliar event *did* develop a momentum of its own, assisted by the optimistic cultural setting of the early 1960s. It was an era dominated by an ideology of 'development' in the social economy, globally speaking, and – despite the Cuban missile crisis of 1962 – an atmosphere of *détente* ('relaxation') between its competing superpowers. Pope John told his former clergy and people in Venice that the Council would further 'clarity of thought and magnanimity of heart'. As optimism turned to hedonism, the Western culture of the 60s encouraged more of the second than the first.

The '*vota*', or aspirations for the Council, expressed by the bishops before coming to Rome ran along markedly different lines from what emerged after they arrived. A number of bishops had wanted, for instance, a condemnation of current philosophical errors, or again, the dogmatic proclamation of further 'privileges' of our Lady, though, to be sure, many of them were already asking for some of the things the Council actually achieved: a clearer definition of the status of the episcopate, the introduction of a permanent married diaconate, a further (no doubt, modest) instalment of the liturgical reform begun by Pope Pius XII. In the upshot, however, the Second Vatican Council left little unchanged in

Catholic life and thought. Its Constitutions, Decrees, and Declarations, especially if taken in conjunction with the liturgical changes introduced when the Council was ended, amount to a 'make-over' of the Church more far-reaching (even) than that attempted at the Council of Trent, which by its reform decrees, and the Catechism and revised liturgical books it commissioned, also sought to re-make the landscape of the Church, and not simply to defend doctrine against the first Protestants.

All in all, then, this was something of a runaway Council which, in the words of the title of a once celebrated book by an English Catholic journalist (appropriately enough, a former Jesuit priest) produced an even more 'runaway Church'. In the years after 1965, appeal to the 'spirit of Vatican II' covered – or, rather, exposed – a multitude of sins. One Orthodox observer remarked in 1985 that the Latin church had turned itself into a 'huge builders' yard – for the worse as well as for the better'. The liturgical abuses and ecumenical excesses, the widespread return to the lay state of Religious and priests, the catechetical confusion, the obfuscation of the distinction between Christian humanism and civil humanism, and the egregious doctrinal deviations which, too often, sheltered behind appeal to the 'Conciliar spirit', were in no way intended by the Council fathers. Honing, in the Council chamber, the letter of the Council's texts was meant to be, precisely, the drawing of a line. But in a vast worldwide communion, where technology rendered communications easy, was the line, in reality, drawn in the sand?

The movement called Catholic Traditionalism, or, less graciously, Lefebvrism, arose in sharp reaction to the post-Conciliar crisis. It is a defensive reaction that wished and wishes to call to a halt what one Conciliar reformer, the distinguished French Oratorian Louis Bouyer, a convert from Calvinism, termed, when he viewed the Council's aftermath, the 'decomposition of Catholicism'. Has Traditionalism chosen the right tools with which to reverse that process of decomposition? If I thought it had, I would presumably join its numbers. But thinking as I do that the initial aims of the Council are perfectly legitimate (and even Mgr Lefebvre baulked at the notion of rejecting the Council 'wholesale'), I prefer to align my own small efforts to consolidate the identity of the Catholic Christian tradition with those of the (spiritually) mighty post-Conciliar Popes, Benedict XVI and John Paul II.

But that is not to say that the Traditionalist critique is unworthy of attention. From the beginning of Mgr Lefebvre's revolt, he played two tunes above all, and very good tunes they are. One is the Sacrifice of the Mass, taken with full seriousness as the renewal of Calvary. The other is the vocation of the Catholic State – the Christendom society. What Traditionalists find unacceptable in the *post-Conciliar settlement* is, first and foremost, the Missal of Paul VI which arises out of the Council but, devised and promulgated after the bishops had returned home, can only be described as mandated by them in a somewhat Pickwickian sense. What Traditionalists find unacceptable in the *Council itself* is, first and foremost, its Declaration on Religious Liberty, which only by rather complex argumentation (they, no doubt, would say, sleight-of-hand) can be squared with the long-standing opposition of the Church to civil recognition, in Catholic countries, of the rights of other religions or irreligions – as distinct from the not only prudent but charitable toleration of those non-Christian world-views and their attendant practices. The post-Conciliar crisis taken *together with* the liturgical reform and the controversial Declaration: these explain, to my mind, Traditionalism's genesis.

What, then, is to be done? Pope Benedict has led the way. Early in 2009 he lifted the excommunications which the bishops consecrated by Mgr Lefebvre had incurred through their uncanonical ordination in 1988. In October 2009, he arranged that a doctrinal dialogue should commence between representatives of the Society of St Pius X and the Pontifical Commission *Ecclesia Dei*. His aim is to reconcile estranged Catholics who have become alienated from the post-Conciliar Church not through contempt or indifference towards the Catholic tradition but, precisely, for the opposite reason, from out of ardent love for it. It goes without saying that a pastor, and especially a universal pastor, will want there to be one flock and one shepherd. It is also the case that the Pope wishes to re-establish in the general conscious-ness of the Church a profound sense of the continuous doctrinal and spiritual identity which joins together the epoch following the Council from the millennia that preceded it. Indeed, we cannot profess belief in the 'one holy, catholic and apostolic Church' of the Creed unless it is so.

For these aims to be realized, the Society – or, more widely, Traditionalists – must be able to discern that continu-ity, and this in turn means that the official Church (in whose name I am taking it upon myself, rather impudently, to speak) must likewise be able to exhibit the continuity in question.

Exactly how that will pan out in the (we gather) difficult dialogue taking place confidentially in Rome is as yet unknown. We do, however, know the agenda – which has been faithfully followed (if occasionally with asides or retro-spective glances) in the letters Moyra Doorly and I have exchanged. Here are the topics, as laid out in a communiqué of 26 October 2009 from the Holy See. They are: the concept of tradition; the Missal of Paul VI; the interpretation of Vatican Council II in continuity with Catholic doctrinal tradition; the theme of the unity of the Church and the Catholic principles of ecumenism, the relationship between Christianity and non-Christian religions, and religious freedom.

The point of view I have taken in the letters is that an orthodox interpretation of both Council and Missal is entirely feasible – which is not to say, however, that either the documents or the book are perfect. In particular there are, I believe, two gaps to fill, two needs that should be met. The first desideratum is a strengthening of the sacrificial element in the Roman Liturgy as contained in the Missal of Paul VI. The second is a statement on the relation of the Church to society which re-affirms the duty of spiritual, moral and cultural leadership that falls to Catholics wherever they are the great majority in any State.

   The letters that follow seek to clarify, then, the great issues at stake in this debate.

Aidan Nichols, OP

The Coming of the Controversy:
The Society's Perspective

In his sermon given at the 1988 Episcopal consecration of four Society of Saint Pius X priests, Archbishop Lefebvre explained how the previous evening, a car had been arranged to take him immediately to Rome as part of a last minute attempt by Pope John Paul II to prevent the ceremony going ahead. In giving his reasons for still being in Ecône, Switzerland, at the SSPX seminary where he intended to proceed as planned, Archbishop Lefebvre declared that day, June 30, to be the beginning of 'Operation Survival' for Tradition and for the Catholic Church.

Anticipating that due to his advanced years, those present would soon be able to read on his tombstone the words of St Paul, 'Tradidi quod et accepi – I have transmitted what I received', Archbishop Lefebvre maintained that since the Second Vatican Council, a change had taken place in the Church which was 'not Catholic' and 'not in conformity with the doctrine of all times'. Despite his desire to be in full union with the Holy Father, he could not accept 'this new spirit which now rules in Rome', and had no choice but to 'continue in Tradition; to keep Tradition while waiting for Tradition to regain its place in Rome, while waiting for Tradition to reassume its place in the Roman authorities, in their minds.' In the meantime, the consecration of bishops was vital if the SSPX was to continue in the face of 'the strong will of the present Roman authorities to reduce Tradition to naught'. Two days later, on 2 July, Pope John Paul II condemned the consecrations as a schismatic act in his Motu Proprio *Ecclesia Dei* and announced the automatic excommunication of those involved. Three years later, at the age of 85, Archbishop Lefebvre died and was buried at Ecône.

Born in 1905 in Tourcoing, north-eastern France, Marcel Lefebvre was the son of factory owner René Lefebvre who died in Sonnenburg concentration camp in 1944 after being arrested by the Nazis for his work with the French Resistance and British Intelligence. Ordained in 1929, Archbishop Lefebvre joined the Holy Ghost Fathers and for the next thirty years followed the life of a missionary and seminary professor in west Africa. Consecrated a bishop in 1947 and made Apostolic Delegate to French-speaking Africa the following year, he was appointed to the Central Preparatory Commission for the Second Vatican Council by Pope John XXIII. In 1962 he was elected Superior General of the Holy Ghost Fathers.

Reporting to his congregation on the progress of the Council, Archbishop Lefebvre expressed deep concern at the direction the liturgical reforms were taking. Viewing collegiality as an attack on the personal power of the pope and of the bishops, which undermined traditional structures, and claiming that a new magisterium was being established, 'the magisterium of public opinion', he voted against the Declaration on Religious Liberty but added his signature to the document. Later he admitted to being unprepared for the determination and influence of the reformers at the Council, and suggested that his thirty years in Africa had kept him out of touch with the movements for modernization so prevalent in Europe during the pre-conciliar period.

Writing to Cardinal Ottaviani in 1966, Archbishop Lefebvre claimed, 'We have lived to see the marriage of the Catholic Church with Liberal ideas.' Finding himself increasingly out of step with those of his congregation who supported the reforms, Archbishop Lefebvre resigned as Superior General in 1968 and the following year, with nine students, established a seminary in Fribourg, Switzerland, with the agreement of Bishop Charrière, who went on to recognize the International Priestly Society of Saint Pius X as a 'pious union', a society of priests without vows. The seminary, which moved to Ecône in 1971, was later described as 'the Wildcat Seminary' by the French bishops, who indicated that they would incardinate none of its seminarians.

In November 1974, Archbishop Lefebvre received notification of an imminent visit by representatives of a commission of cardinals set up by the Holy Father. Two days later, the Apostolic Visitors arrived and after their departure, in a mood he later described as being of 'doubtlessly excessive indignation', Archbishop Lefebvre made the soon to be much criticized 'Declaration' to his seminarians, in which he claimed that the conciliar reforms were responsible for 'the destruction of the Church, the ruin of the priesthood, the abolishing of the sacrifice of the Mass and of the Sacraments, the disappearance of the religious life'. Insisting that 'no authority, not even the highest in the hierarchy, can force us to abandon or diminish our Catholic Faith, clearly laid down and professed by the magisterium of the Church for nineteen hundred years,' he concluded that, 'the only attitude of fidelity to the Church and to Catholic doctrine appropriate for our salvation is a categorical refusal to accept this reformation.'

Summoned to Rome twice the following year and reproached for his 'Declaration', Archbishop Lefebvre then received news of the suppression of the SSPX and the Ecône seminary, which by then had 104 seminarians and 13 professors. Insisting that the correct procedures had not been followed and that he had been given no opportunity to defend himself, Archbishop Lefebvre went ahead with the priestly ordinations of 1976 and was suspended *a divinis*. Among his many writings and addresses, that year Archbishop Lefebvre published *I Accuse the Council*, in which he explained the Interventions he made during each of the four sessions of Vatican II. And in 1985, *Religious Liberty Questioned* was delivered to the Sacred Congregation for the Doctrine of the Faith at the request of the then Cardinal Ratzinger.

To understand the difference between the SSPX and other priestly societies who celebrate the pre-conciliar liturgy but are reconciled with Rome, it is useful to look at the Protocol Archbishop Lefebvre signed during a meeting with Cardinal Ratzinger shortly before the 1988 consecrations. Although he quickly withdrew his support for the document, this Protocol was proposed by Pope John Paul II in *Ecclesia Dei*, as the basis for the reconciliation with Rome of 'priests, seminarians, religious communities, or individuals until now linked in various ways to the Fraternity founded by Archbishop Lefebvre'. Those priestly societies which accept the Protocol are therefore committed to its paragraph 1(3) provision, which insists on 'avoiding all polemics' regarding 'points taught by the Second Vatican Council or concerning later reforms of the liturgy and law, and which seem to us able to be reconciled with Tradition only with difficulty'. Thus those who celebrate the traditional liturgy and are reconciled with Rome are effectively prohibited from criticizing the Council, a position the SSPX could not contemplate.

As the Holy Father Pope Benedict pointed out in his letter of March 12, 2009, concerning the lifting of the excommunications against Bishop Bernard Fellay, Bishop Tissier de Mallerais, Bishop Richard Williamson and Bishop Alfonso de Galarreta, 'the problems now to be addressed are essentially doctrinal in nature'. Meanwhile the SSPX has grown to include 491 priests, 215 seminarians, 117 brothers, 164 sisters and thousands of Catholic supporters across the world who maintain, as Archbishop Lefebvre did, that the Council is the problem, not the manner in which it has been interpreted and implemented. According to *The Problem of the Liturgical Reform: A Theological and Liturgical Study* published in 2001 by the SSPX, the Second Vatican Council and its reforms have introduced a new understanding of the Mass, one that is, 'less an application of the merits of Redemption and more a liturgy of the saved – the liturgy of a *people your Son has gained for you*. Rather than being an action whereby the priest *in persona Christi* applies the merits and satisfactions won by Christ in His redemptive sacrifice, the Mass is the action of a people – "the sacred assembly, a chosen race, a royal priesthood" – who celebrate with thanksgiving a Redemption already released in full'.

The following correspondence between Aidan Nichols, OP, and myself began as a single exchange of letters intended for publication in the UK's *Catholic Herald*. Therefore while there are six items on the agenda for the doctrinal discussions between the Vatican and the Society of Saint Pius X, the series here includes seven letter exchanges, the first two covering topics likely to be discussed under the heading 'The Missal of Pope Paul VI', and the remaining five following the agenda as listed. Hopefully, this exercise will be of some assistance in the task of breaking down the barriers which define the current situation.

Moyra Doorly

First Letter from a Confused Catholic: On the Reform of the Roman Liturgy

May 2009

Dear Fr Aidan,

The current orthodoxy is that the liturgical crisis in the Church is the result not of the Second Vatican Council itself, but of the manner in which it has been implemented. Unfortunately, this reminds me of how western communists reacted when the reality of life in the Soviet Union became apparent. Karl Marx's ideas were not at fault, they insisted. The problem, instead, was how they had been put into practice.

This may be an analogy too far. But when the modernist architects sold their vision of cities fit for a brave, new machine age, and the vision turned out to look like the Peckham Estate, now demolished, their response was to blame not their own ideas, but the governments and local authorities who had cut corners and skimped on the details. And so too the undoubting feminists, who wanted to liberate women from the shackles of patriarchal marriage and establish a nurturing, sharing matriarchy which, in the real world, meant children without fathers.

Given that the twentieth century produced so many silver-tongued visionaries determined to sweep away the past and remake the world, could the liturgical renewal simply be another example of a big idea gone wrong? And could the current liturgical crisis actually stem from the Council itself, which articulated the vision? One clue is to be found in the Foreword to the 2005 edition of the *General Instruction on the Roman Missal* (para. 2), which asserts that Vatican II reaffirmed the sacrificial nature of the Mass as affirmed by the Council of Trent in accordance with the Church's universal tradition. The *GIRM* then refers to the *Constitution on the Sacred Liturgy* (para. 47) which states,

> At the Last Supper, on the night he was betrayed, our Saviour instituted the eucharistic sacrifice of his Body and Blood. This he did in order to perpetuate the sacrifice of the Cross throughout the ages until he should come again, and so to entrust to his beloved Spouse, the Church, a memorial of his death and resurrection: a sacrament of love, a sign of unity, a bond of charity, a paschal banquet in which Christ is consumed, the mind is filled with grace, and a pledge of future glory is given to us.

But compare this with an apparently similar, but significantly different, definition of the Mass in Pope Pius XII's 1947 Encyclical *Mediator Dei* (para. 67),

> Christ the Lord, Eternal Priest according to the order of Melchisedech, loving His own who were of the world, at the last supper, on the night He was betrayed, wishing to leave His beloved Spouse, the Church, *a visible sacrifice such as the nature of men requires,* that would re-present the bloody sacrifice offered once on the cross, and perpetuate its memory to the end of time, *and whose salutary virtue might be applied in remitting those sins which we daily commit* ... offered His body and blood under the species of bread and wine to God the Father, and under the same species allowed the apostles, whom He at that time constituted the priests of the New Testament, to partake thereof; commanding them and their successors in the priesthood to make the same offering. (my emphasis)

Somehow the propitiatory character of the sacrifice of the Mass has been dropped from the *CSL* version, with the emphasis placed on a 'bond of charity, a paschal banquet', etc., and the Mass is described as a memorial of Christ's 'death and resurrection'.

In Part II, Chapter 4 of the *Catechism of the Council of Trent*, the various terms used to 'convey the dignity and excellence of this admirable sacrament' are explained, e.g. the Eucharist, the Sacrifice, Communion, the sacrament of peace and charity, the supper. (Q 3-5) Also explained are the three things indicated by this sacrament,

> The first is the Passion of Christ the Lord, a thing past ... Another is divine and heavenly grace which, being present, is imparted by this sacrament, to nurture and preserve the soul ... The third thing, which it foreshows as future, is the fruit of eternal joy and glory which, according to God's promise, we shall receive in our heavenly country. (Q11)

But no room is left to doubt that

> the Eucharist was instituted by Christ for two purposes, one, that it might be the celestial food of our soul, by which we may be able to support and preserve life; the other, that the Church might have a perpetual sacrifice, by which our sins might be expiated. (Q 68)

And also that,

> it must be unhesitatingly taught that ... the holy sacrifice of the Mass is not a sacrifice of praise and thanksgiving only, or a mere commemoration of the sacrifice accomplished on the cross, but also a truly propitiatory sacrifice, by which God is appeased and rendered propitious to us. (Q 76)

As far as I can make out, this is because, '... Christ, after redeeming the world at the lavish cost of His own blood, still must come into complete possession of the souls of men.' So states *Mediator Dei* (para. 77), which continues,

> In a certain sense it can be said that on Calvary Christ built a font of purification and salvation which He filled with the blood He shed; but if men do not bathe in it and there wash away the sins of their iniquities, they can never be purified or saved.

To be fair, the *GIRM* (Foreword, para. 2) does include the following: 'The Mass is a sacrifice of praise, of thanksgiving, of propitiation and of satisfaction.' But then it goes on to practically ignore this, as do the rest of the Council documents. Everywhere the emphasis is on the Mass as a memorial of Christ's Death, Resurrection and Ascension – the Paschal Mystery – which the people gather to celebrate as if Salvation is guaranteed because God's love is unconditional and His justice makes no demands.

For example the *CSL* (para. 5) points out that:

> The wonderful works of God among the people of the Old Testament were but a prelude to the work of Christ Our Lord in redeeming mankind and giving perfect glory to God. He achieved his task principally by the paschal mystery of his blessed passion, resurrection from the dead, and glorious ascension . . .

And continues (para. 6), 'the Church has never failed to come together to celebrate the paschal mystery, reading those things "which were in all the scriptures concerning him, celebrating the Eucharist" . . .' And then sums up with (para. 106),

> . . . the Church celebrates the paschal mystery every eighth day, which day is appropriately called the Lord's Day or Sunday. For on this day Christ's faithful are bound to come together into one place. They should listen to the word of God and take part in the Eucharist, thus calling to mind the passion, resurrection and glory of the Lord Jesus . . .

Which is all very puzzling. What's more, something seems to have happened to the teaching on the priesthood. According to the *Dogmatic Constitution on the Church* (para. 10),

> Though they differ essentially and not only in degree, the common priesthood of the faithful and the ministerial

priesthood are none the less ordered to one another; each in its own proper way shares in the one priesthood of Christ ... The faithful indeed, by virtue of their royal priesthood, participate in the offering of the Eucharist ...

And the *Decree on the Ministry and Life of Priests* (para. 5), has this to say:

> The purpose then for which priests are consecrated to God through the ministry of the bishop is that they should be made sharers in a special way in Christ's priesthood ... the eucharistic celebration is the centre of the assembly of the faithful over which the priest presides. Hence priests teach the faithful to offer the divine victim to God the Father in the sacrifice of the Mass and with the victim to make an offering of their whole life.

Does this mean that the laity and the ordained priesthood share in the one priesthood of Christ, albeit 'each in its own proper way'? As *Mediator Dei* points out, the priesthood was instituted at the Last Supper. Am I right in thinking that this was achieved without the presence of the lay faithful?

On this subject, according to the *Catechism of the Council of Trent*'s definition (ch 7, q 2),

> ... the priests of the new testament far excel all others in honour; for the power of consecrating and offering the body and blood of our Lord, and of remitting sins, which has been conferred on them, transcends human reason and intelligence, still less can there be found on earth anything equal and like to it.

And yet somehow, the priest has now become the 'president of the assembly'.

It is hardly worth quoting the Council documents on their by now familiar proposals for reforming the appearance of the liturgy. But since the reforms were intended to encourage the people to participate actively and as a unity in the Mass, and to this end the rites were simplified and the non-authentic and therefore disposable accumulations of the centuries stripped away to reveal an underlying purity and simplicity, the question is whether or not these proposals could ever have been suggested, far less put into practice, had there not been a shift in thinking on the nature of the Mass and the Priesthood.

If 'form follows function' as the architect Mies van der Rohe claimed, then the appearance and structure of the Ordinary Form of the Roman Rite will resemble a community gathering and a fraternal meal, because its function is considered to be just that. Similarly, the Extraordinary Form will appear as a sacrificial rite because sacrifice is considered its primary aim.

Therefore the current attempts to 'reform the reform' by adding more Latin and Gregorian chant, or discouraging Communion in the hand and replacing the sanctuary rails, will not be able to overcome the fundamental opposition that the Ordinary Form has to these additions, since they are, essentially, superfluous to its requirements. After all, if the people are almost priests, why shouldn't they receive Communion in the hand?

Since a rationalised, stripped down, community-orientated liturgy is bound to become desacralised, rather than tinker with the appearances, surely the question has to be addressed – what was the mindset that allowed this vision of liturgical renewal to take hold in the first place?

Kindest regards,
Moyra

A First Reply to a Confused Catholic

Dear Moyra,

Thank you so much for your letter. You express – in a very lucid fashion! – your sense of confusion arising from the study you have been making of the life of the Church. That concerns especially the worshipping Church which, as we know, has changed greatly in the last forty or so years. For the sake of anyone else who may be reading this exchange of letters, I should give a reminder of the context (my introductory essay sketches out the background as I see it). Pope Benedict is seeking to regularize canonically the situation of bishops, priests, religious and laity belonging to the Society of St Pius X. That will not be possible without a resolution of the difficulties those fellow Catholics encounter when they consider the Second Vatican Council, its documents and its aftermath. And that in turn is the departure-point of my reply to this, and subsequent, letters from you.

As a Catholic journalist, you set yourself the task of investigating the nature of the charges the Society brings against the more recent teaching and practice of the Church. You then found yourself in a degree of sympathy with the objectors, based in part on your own earlier researches into changing styles in twentieth-century church architecture, with their by no means always happy consequences for the ethos of the Liturgy. So your letter to me focuses on the accusations Traditionalists level at the documents of the Council (and subsequent teaching instruments like the *General Instruction on the Roman Missal*).

Their claim is that these official texts fail to do justice to the central act of the Church's worship, which is the Mass, the sacrament of the saving Sacrifice of our great High Priest, now offered in a bloodless fashion (indeed, at Christ's own insistence, through the oblation of food and drink) by the hands of the sacerdotal celebrant, the Church's minister. The source of your confusion is this. It is not clear how to respond to these objections in a way that is persuasive because it is the truth.

May I preface my remark by an attempt at capturing the objectors' sympathies? Traditionalists and ourselves are surely in agreement that the forms of the Church's worship have developed over time, not only by incremental changes so slow and anonymous as hardly to be registered by contemporaries but, on occasion, through sharp interventions from above. But this has never previously taken place in the wholesale and systematic fashion which characterized the reform of the Missal, the rites of the remaining sacraments, and the other offices of the Church, undertaken by Pope Paul VI. You, Moyra, will probably support me when I say that the scale of this reform, even had its components been entirely felicitous, was imprudently chosen, since of its nature liturgical life has to strike people as *something that happens*, not as *something that is planned*. In the Latin church, in countries like our own, the effects have been at times deeply disorienting, as is obvious to someone coming into the Church (like myself) in the 1960s, and is readily discovered by the inquiring mind of a convert of later date (such as yourself). One of the principal sufferers has been the sense of the Holy Eucharist as a sacrificial act, since the combined effect of textual, ritual and architectural changes (by the latter I have in mind the almost universal adoption of celebration facing the people) has been – unintentionally, of course – to weaken the sense that this sacrament is the renewed Calvary of the Church's oblation. And this is especially so when these changes are underpinned (as, unfortunately, is often the case) by a catechesis which prefers to

concentrate virtually unilaterally on the more easily assimil-
able theme of the Eucharistic banquet, the Eucharistic meal.

But now perhaps I shall surprise you by saying that I find
the contrasts you draw between the earlier and later texts
you are comparing to be unnecessarily sharp. Let me take
first your worries about the doctrine of the Mass, and subse-
quently turn my attention to the theology of priesthood. On
the first of these two great subjects, I must begin by saying I
do not think it is good theology to place an account of the
Atoning Sacrifice of the God-Man *over against* a description
of the Paschal Mystery. The term 'the Paschal Mystery' simply
refers to the Atoning Sacrifice as not *only offered by the Son*
in the Holy Spirit (compare Hebrews 9:14), the Spirit who is
personally the Love of the Father and the Son but, furthermore, as *accepted by the Father* in that same Spirit. The form
the acceptance of the Sacrifice took is the Son's
Resurrection, Ascension, and Seating at the Father's right,
there to pour forth forever the salvation he has won for us.

Similarly, I do not think it is plausible to *contrast* a
Eucharistic theology of propitiation and supplication with a
teaching on the unity, charity, and peace made available to us
through communion in the Eucharistic Gifts. The Eucharistic
Gifts are the Spotless Lamb whose offering is renewed in the
Sacrifice of the altar. The unity, charity and peace involved
are the communication to us of a share-by-participation in
the Trinitarian life from that same Christ who made the
perfect Oblation for us once and for all. In each case –
the once-for-all Sacrifice and its sacramental re-enactment
– the mercy and pardon made available to sinners through
Christ's Passion cannot be separated from the gifts of
communion in his Resurrection life: both are the fruit of his
endlessly meritorious work on the Cross. The Mass is often
called 'The Eucharist', meaning 'The Thanksgiving', not in
order to deflect attention from its propitiatory and satisfactory aspects but so as to underline that in the Mass we
render thanks for these blessings *in their total ensemble*.

Duly pondered, these doctrinal principles should indicate the basic continuity between the two sets of text to which you appeal: the *Catechism of the Council of Trent* and Pius XII's *Mediator Dei* on the one hand, and the *Constitution on the Sacred Liturgy* and the *General Instruction on the Roman Missal* (third typical edition) on the other.

The massive attendance which is still normal at the Good Friday Liturgy indicates, I suggest, that the sense of the faithful remains fundamentally sound on the topic of the saving Sacrifice. We have not become an 'Easter people' in the pejorative sense of that phrase for which the Death of Christ is only the prelude to Resurrection rejoicing. Sunday is the weekly Easter, but that is because the triumph of the Cross can only be fully viewed from the side of the Resurrection. It is not because the Cross and the Tomb are put away as Saturday night draws near. Even a Sunday Mass – or, rather (I have to correct myself) *especially* a Sunday Mass – should be focused on the all-sufficient Sacrifice, because only that Sacrifice made Easter possible. That is why we need to work on not only catechesis but also, in the fullness of time, a revision of the Offertory texts, the cere-monial of the Mass, and (not least) the position of the celebrant, so as to re-activate the diminished, but by no means extinguished, feeling of the faithful for the sacramen-tal identity of Calvary and the Eucharist of the Church.

The things you mention that would increase reverence (the chant, kneeling communion, communion on the tongue) are not strictly necessary accompaniments of the Mass (the Eastern churches, for instance, stand to receive), but they are congruent with the demands of the Mass (every Mass, so including those in the *Novus Ordo*).

Reference to the Mass celebrant brings me to the other major point you raise, Moyra, and this concerns the relative position (theologically speaking, and not just spatially considered) of priest and people. Two key words in the explanation of Catholic doctrine, frequent in the Fathers and first enunciated, in fact, in the Scriptures, are 'analogy' and 'participation'. They are, I find, helpful in this context.

You are correct to say that the ministerial priesthood of the ordained and the royal and universal priesthood of the baptized are two distinct yet related ('analogous') ways of sharing ('participating') in the priesthood of Christ. The universal priesthood is exercised most obviously in the good works which should embody faith throughout the Christian life. But that general priesthood also has a cultic dimension. Just as it was begun for the faithful in the sacramental mysteries of Baptism, so it finds its noblest expression in their Eucharistic worship. At Mass, the baptized exercise their royal priesthood because, in Pope Pius's terminology (see *Mediator Dei* 88), they are 'members of the Mystical Body of Christ the Priest', while the Head of that Body represents himself to them in the ministerial priest who, like Christ, stands before the Father on their behalf. The ordained minister's analogical participation in Christ's High Priesthood is, accordingly, different from that of the lay faithful. The latter can offer the (as yet, unconsecrated) gifts in a properly Eucharistic way only through the hands of the ministerial priest – though once those gifts have become, through the act which is his by the New Covenant sealed at the Supper, the Body and Blood of the Lamb, the people co-offer with the priest the saving Victim to the Father.

Were there, you ask me, laypeople in the Cenacle at the Last Supper? I have to answer that I don't know. But I do know that in the High Priestly Prayer recorded from that Supper in the Gospel of St John, the Saviour prays that the apostolic priesthood may truly be consecrated so that a wider flock may be gathered into their company (John 17:19–21). Every Mass, even when celebrated by a hermit priest in the desert, is offered in the name of the whole Church: not only validly but fruitfully for the living and the dead. The Mass of the hermit is a moving testimony to the unseen. Yet the mystery of the Mass finds its true liturgical epiphany when it is celebrated with the holy people of God. Notice I incorporate within the phrase 'people of God' the adjective 'holy', as in the Latin original of the term (*plebs sancta Dei*), since in divine arithmetic mere demonstration of numbers signifies nothing.

The Liturgy is, normatively, an assembly (the case of the hermit is exceptional). But it is the sort of assembly described in the Letter to the Hebrews (12:22–24), which includes the angels and saints and, as its centre, the 'sprinkled blood' of the 'Mediator' which 'speaks more graciously than the blood of Abel'. Unless we can insinuate that *this* is the assembly we have in mind, let us have done with the language of the ordained priest as 'president'. Otherwise, what a word! Insipid, bureaucratic, jejune.

I hope, Moyra, that your search will be helped by these comments and that you in turn will help others to find the fullness of the faith.

Yours sincerely,
Fr Aidan

Second Letter from a Confused Catholic: On the Eucharistic Doctrine of the Missal of Pope Paul VI

August 2009

Dear Fr Aidan,

In your kind reply to my first letter you made the point that I was drawing 'unnecessarily sharp' contrasts between a theology of 'propitiation and supplication' on one hand, and teachings on the 'fruits of Communion' on the other. But what I was trying to demonstrate is that the pre-Conciliar sources give ample teaching on both, whereas the documents of Vatican II ignore the theology of propitiation and supplication.

Now to me this represents a doctrinal discontinuity of the first order, and may explain my long held suspicion that the Church since Vatican II seems intent on bypassing Golgotha and heading straight for Pentecost. And yet we are told repeatedly that no such discontinuity exists. What's more, even the suggestion that it might, will be met from many quarters with threats of exile in the gulag along with the Society of Saint Pius X who hold the view, as expressed in the November 2006 newsletter of their Holy Cross Seminary, Australia, that 'the New Mass is a grave danger to the Catholic Faith ... it lacks the integral profession of Faith that is essential to the Sacred Liturgy'.

It may be possible to explain the contrast between the appearances of the Ordinary and Extraordinary Forms – how they look, sound, and are experienced – by pointing to the Council's desire for the active participation of the laity as announced by the *Constitution on the Sacred Liturgy* (para. 14), 'In the restoration and promotion of the sacred liturgy the full and active participation by all the people is the aim to be considered before all else'. But then another discontinuity becomes apparent, since according to Pope Pius XII's Encyclical *Mediator Dei* (para. 23, 24), 'The Worship rendered by the Church to God must be, in its entirety, interior as well as exterior ... But the chief element of divine worship must be interior.'

Alternatively the finger may be pointed at over-enthusiastic modernisers who have taken the liturgy in directions previously undreamt of. But according to the CSL (para. 37), 'Even in the liturgy the Church does not wish to impose a rigid conformity in matters which do not involve the faith or the good of the whole community.' And (para. 40), 'In some places and circumstances, however, an even more radical adaptation of the liturgy is needed'.

What puzzles me is that despite the extent of the current crisis in the Church, no-one seems prepared to question Vatican II itself. Instead the insistence is upon liturgical changes not mandated by the Council and less than adequate catechetics. Although defined as pastoral and not dogmatic, Vatican II is considered to be beyond criticism.

Except by the SSPX, whose founder Archbishop Lefebvre wrote in *A Bishop Speaks: Writings and Addresses 1963–1976* (Angelus Press),

> the sacrifice of the Mass is the heart, the soul, and the mystical wellspring of the Church ... Do not the ills of the Church, the weakening of faith, the dwindling number of vocations, the destruction of religious communities ... spring from the doing away with altars and their replacement by the tables of the Eucharistic meal?

Could it possibly be that the Council sidelined certain teachings in order to achieve the aim, professed in the CSL (para. 4), that the liturgy be revised 'to meet present-day circumstances and needs'? Is this why we never hear the traditional teaching that while Christ redeemed the human race, salvation requires the sacrifice of the altar for the remission of the sins we daily commit and the individual's cooperation with grace? And why the impression now given is that Christ's death on the Cross was a once and for all sacrifice by which all are saved, and that the Eucharist is spiritual food for those guaranteed a place in heaven through faith? Is this easier, softer way intended to be more in tune with the modern age which exalts man and rejects sacrifice?

Could it be that the reforms inspired by the documents of Vatican II have resulted in a liturgy which is inherently incapable of expressing the true sacrificial character of the Mass? If I am hammering a point previously made, here is Archbishop Lefebvre again: 'There is no longer a Catholic Church if there is no longer a sacrifice of the Mass. There is no longer a Catholic Church if there is no longer a priest endowed with a character for the offering of the holy sacrifice.'

At any rate, if the Holy Sacrifice of the Mass has become a memorial meal, a fraternal banquet, a community gathering, then many features of the reformed liturgy are explained. It is natural at a memorial meal for the priest to face the people who 'gather round' an altar which has become a table. It makes sense that the people take an active part in simplified rites celebrated in the vernacular.

Although not actually mandating Mass facing the people, the CSL (para. 128) opened the door for it by announcing the abolition of laws governing the design of churches, the shape and construction of altars and the placing of the tabernacle 'which seem less suited to the reformed liturgy'. Similarly, while permitting the vernacular with the proviso that 'care must be taken to ensure that the faithful may also be able to say or sing together in Latin those parts of the Ordinary of the Mass which pertain to them', the CSL (para. 54) also anticipated situations in which 'a more extended use of the vernacular in the Mass seems desirable.'

In this context, the scope given for liturgical variations and innovations also seems natural, although this too represents a discontinuity according to the series *SiSi NoNo* published in the SSPX's *Angelus* magazine, March 2003, which claims that,

> Vatican II promoted the adaptation of worship to secular culture, to the different traditions and temperaments of people, to their language, music, and art, through creativity and liturgical experimentation and through simplification of the rite itself. This was against the constant teaching of the Magisterium according to which it was the peoples' cultures that must adapt to the exigencies of the Catholic rite, with nothing ever having been conceded to creativity or experimentation or to any idea of men's temperaments in any given time in history.

A proposal currently gaining ground is that the Ordinary Form be re-sacralised, implying that the liturgical tendencies of the past 40 years are a matter of appearances only. But is the Ordinary Form a true sacrificial rite? Not according to the SSPX study *The Problem of the Liturgical Reform*, which claims that the reforms have diminished the traditional link between the Mass and the Cross in favour of the Last Supper.

To this end, the traditional Prayers at the Foot of the Altar have been replaced with simple Introductory Rites. The traditional Offertory with its unstinting emphasis on propitiatory sacrifice has become the Presentation of the Gifts which emphasizes the peoples' offering of bread and wine which will become 'the bread of life' and 'our spiritual drink'. The Last Gospel has been dropped, as have the traditional anthems to the Blessed Virgin Mary.

Furthermore, the presence of Christ in Scripture is made

equivalent to His True Presence on the altar. For example the CSL (para. 48) states that the people, 'should be instructed by God's word, and be nourished at the table of the Lord's Body'. And that the people (para. 106), 'should listen to the word of God and take part in the Eucharist'. So marked is the emphasis on Scripture in the Ordinary Form, that the Liturgy of the Eucharist can sometimes seem like an adjunct to the main proceedings, with every prayer spoken out loud contributing to the relentless din of amplified voices.

The Study also claims that the gestures showing the respect intrinsic to a truly sacrificial rite have also been reduced in number or suppressed. For example, 'of the 14 genuflections in the traditional missal, three alone have been kept'. And, 'of the 26 signs of the cross over the oblations in the canon of the traditional missal, one alone remains in each of the Eucharistic prayers'. And so on.

Is it enough, then, to re-sacralise the Ordinary Form, to adjust its appearance without addressing its underlying form and structure as a memorial meal? Should it not, instead, be *re-sacrificialised?*

Or in the words of Archbishop Lefebvre,

Perhaps there has been too much talk of the Eucharist, Communion, and not enough of the sacrifice of the Mass. I believe we should go back to the fundamental ideas, to that fundamental idea which has been that of the whole tradition of the Church, the Sacrifice of the Mass, which is the heart of the Church. Communion is but the fruit, the fruit of the sacrifice . . .

Kindest regards,
Moyra

A Second Reply to a Confused Catholic

Dear Moyra,

Thank you for your recent letter, in which you ask for further clarification about the sacrificial nature of the Mass and add some pointed remarks about certain weaknesses in the Rite of Paul VI, the Eucharistic Liturgy most of us in the West experience weekly or even daily – with a familiarity which justifies that rather dull expression the 'Ordinary Form'. (Not that, to normal users of English, 'Extraordinary' sounds any better!)

Pace threats of 'exile in the gulag', you are not a disloyal Catholic by dint of holding that a number of the measures the Council fathers called for by way of liturgical revision offended against prudence. Naturally, a judgment of that kind is easier to make with the benefit of hindsight, but warning lights should surely have flashed when a blank cheque was offered to national episcopal conferences and the Roman dicasteries to make radical changes in the name of cultural adaptation, which is what happened in *Sacrosanctum Concilium* 40 (though the word 'radical', I hasten to add, appears only in English translation, since the Latin original reads, when literally translated, 'deeper and more difficult'). Prudential judgments about what practical steps to take so as best to realize goals indicated by the teaching of the Church about faith and morals are not covered, unfortunately, by the inspiration of the Holy Ghost.

Again, you are not a 'dissenter' simply by criticizing incomplete or unbalanced formulations in the language of the Conciliar texts. That is wholly different from the claim that the Council fathers formally committed the Church to doctrinal error.

And that brings me to the substance of your remarks. Reading through the sections of the Liturgy Constitution that concern the Mass, I am inclined to agree with you that an opportunity was missed to spell out the 'ends' – the purposes – of the Mass considered as Sacrifice. Not that *Sacrosanctum Concilium* fails to make plain the sacrificial nature of the Eucharist. In language which would surely be anathema to the Protestant Reformers, it declares flatly that 'our Saviour instituted the Eucharistic Sacrifice of his Body and Blood ... in order to perpetuate the Sacrifice of the Cross throughout the centuries until he should come again' (para. 47), and adds a few sentences later that 'offering the Immaculate Victim, ... [Christ's faithful] should learn to offer themselves too' (para. 48). I can hardly underline too strongly how distasteful these expressions must be to well-informed and committed Lutherans, Calvinists, and Evangelicals generally. Nevertheless, more could have been said along the lines that you (and the Society of St Pius X) desiderate.

For some centuries it has been the common teaching of theologians, widely publicized in catechisms, that the Mass, viewed as Sacrifice, has a quartet of purposes. It is a Sacrifice of praise and thanksgiving, propitiation and supplication. The grounds for making this claim are that these are the very aims of our Lord's own giving of himself at the first Easter. His Death was an Offering whereby he glorified the Father (thanksgiving and praise) in such a way as to secure pardon (propitiation) and help (supplication) for humankind. Precisely because the Mass-Sacrifice is, as Vatican II maintains, the perpetuation of the Sacrifice of the Cross, it can have no other ends than had the act performed on the Tree.

Appreciating that fact should discourage us from racing over what we might consider the 'soft' and Protestantism-compatible theme of praise and thanksgiving in order to get as quickly as possible to the 'tough' and more distinctively Tridentine-sounding motifs of propitiation and supplication. Our doctrine is not that the Holy Eucharist is a 'sacrifice of praise' in some vague sense equally applicable to any other worshipping activity and so perfectly acceptable to Reformation Christians. The Mass is a 'sacrifice of praise' first and foremost *in the sense in which Calvary was and because Calvary was.*

A good theology will seek to inter-relate the four ends of the Mass, as likewise the ends of the Atonement, in an integrated doctrine, and I doubt if a better one can be found than that for which the Sacrifice of the Lord is a 'latreutic' Sacrifice (from the Greek *latreutikos*, which means 'pertaining to divine worship'), a Sacrifice of adoration in which the Son, invested with our nature, glorifies the Father in the Holy Spirit. It is through being its own unique offering of praise and thanksgiving, in the unmeasured donation of his dying, that the Son's Oblation as man won for the human race super-abundant pardon and help. The proof that a theology of glorification provides the best way to inter-relate the ends of the Mass lies in the nature of the pardon and help we are to receive through the offering of this Sacrifice. We are to become not just reconciled sinners, in receipt of spiritual (and sometimes temporal) assistance. More than that, we are to become those who, in the words of the Vulgate translation of the Letter to the Ephesians (1:12) live for 'the praise of [God's] glory'.

Evidently, the subject of the Mass as a propitiatory Sacrifice is your principal concern. Even for 'post-Conciliar' Catholics, the Mass as a Sacrifice of supplication is not so difficult an idea. Among those assisting at the rite of Paul VI, not many worshippers can be unaware that in the Holy Eucharist petition is made, in our Redeemer's name, for the bestowal of spiritual and temporal good – though, I would emphasize, such 'supplication' should always be understood in a

Calvary-oriented way, as mercies flowing from the Throne of grace established on the Cross. Propitiation, however, is a different kettle of fish. Your anxiety is that, in the reformed rite, insufficient attention is paid to our need for remission of sins (sins that, rightly, have offended God's burning justice) through, precisely, the offering of the Holy Sacrifice of the altar. A really *Catholic* liturgical form will indeed be concerned with propitiation in and through the Mass – though, as I have emphasized, that theme will be suitably interwoven with those of praise, thanksgiving and supplication in a latreutic unity.

But let us be absolutely clear what we are talking about when we speak of the Mass as a propitiatory Sacrifice. As a well-instructed Catholic, you will know that the chief sacramental means provided for the forgiveness of sins are the Sacrament of Baptism (for original sin, as well as the personal sins of adults approaching Christian initiation) and (for post-Baptismal sin) the Sacrament of Penance. Extra-sacramentally, sin can only be forgiven through perfect contrition – sorrow for sin for the sake of the sheer love-ableness of God. When we say the Mass is a Sacrifice of propitiation, we are not saying that the offering of the Mass forgives mortal sin (grave sin) directly, though we may hold that a good Communion covers minor slackenings (venial sins) in the Christian life. We are saying that the Holy Sacrifice wins for us – and for all for whom it is offered, including, most especially indeed, the souls in Purgatory – those graces which render repentance, contrition, full conversion, not only possible but even easy. It would take a detailed analysis of the Proper prayers of the Missal of Paul VI to justify the claim, but my estimate is you would find that expectation represented there, though not, it is true, so insistently as in the earlier history of the rites. (An example from that Missal, the 'Prayer over the Gifts' for Sunday XXV *per Annum*, reads, when literally translated, 'Propitiated, Lord, accept, we beseech you, the offerings of your people', for these offerings – this is the prayer's undoubted assumption – are to become the sole Oblation that *can* propitiate, the sacrificial self-offering of the Son made man.)

That said, I would agree with you on this score: we need to 're-sacrificialize', in your invented but useful word, our common or garden usage of the rite of Paul VI – if not, in some respects (I have in mind chiefly the Offertory prayers), the rite itself. But to my mind the single greatest contribution we can make to that end is to press – judiciously and with respect – for the celebration of the Mass *versus orientem*, the Liturgy 'turned towards the Lord'. The celebrant stands ministerially in the place of Christ the High Priest. Appropriately, since our Great High Priest is Mediator between God and men, the Church's priest, during the Liturgy of the Sacrifice (after, namely, the litany-like moment of the Bidding Prayers) turns at key moments to the body of the faithful, engaging their response to the sacred action of which he is protagonist. (I might mention here that 'active' participation means *engaged* participation, not jumping up and down!) Essentially, however, in the celebration of the Sacrifice the ministerial priest is turned – *always* in spiritual attitude if, in our current practice, seldom in empirical fact – *not* to face the people but, with the beloved Son, to face the Father, to whom the Oblation of praise and thanksgiving, propitiation and supplication is addressed. Your desire for a clearer indication of the change in level as we move from the Liturgy of the Word to the Liturgy of the Sacrifice would be well met by the change of direction whereby the priest, at that shift in gear, turns from facing the people to facing the Father. A strengthening of the Offertory rite would appropriately accompany that alteration in our ceremonial practice.

Your other complaints I find rather a mixed bag. The suppression of the multiple signs of the Cross is a loss for the personal piety of the celebrant rather than the people to whom – with an oriented Liturgy – they would not be so apparent. I personally regret the suppression of the Last Gospel because, in my view, people cannot hear too often the Johannine Prologue which is almost always the form that Gospel takes (though you became a Catholic too late to witness the disedifying scurrying out of church by half the parish congregation as it was read). I don't think there has been any significant reduction in Marian references from one Missal to the other, for the simple reason that the Roman Liturgy, unlike the Byzantine, has always been sparing of reference to the Mother of God except on her feasts and commemorations.

Not that I wish to make light of your plea. All is not well in our worship, and you are right to be concerned. Concerned – but not alarmist. This or that version of the Church's official worship may have, compared with some other, ritual deficiencies which should be rectified as soon as the competent authority is convinced of the case. Meanwhile, we can rest assured that where the Holy Spirit *does* guide the Church is in ensuring that in her approach to the mystery of Christ she can never nullify the stream of grace not only continually but continuously poured from his opened Heart. Our confidence in the Church turns crucially on that conviction. May it always be ours.

Yours ever,
Fr Aidan

Third Letter from a Confused Catholic: On the Idea of Tradition

November 2009

Dear Fr Aidan,

'We are ready to write the Creed with our own blood', wrote SSPX Bishop Fellay in his December 15, 2008 letter to Cardinal Castrillon Hoyos. Now I don't know about anyone else, Fr Aidan, but to me this assertion is almost heart-stopping. After all, when was the last time in this apathetic and lukewarm age that a man of the Church spoke in such terms?

I mention this because the subject here is 'The Concept of Tradition', the first topic being discussed between the SSPX and Rome. And also because it is the SSPX's adherence to Tradition, they claim, that has led to their estrangement from a Rome imbued with the spirit of liberalism and modernism embraced by the Second Vatican Council and imposed on the Catholic faithful following the Council.

In his 1988 *Motu Propio, Ecclesia Dei Afflicta* (para. 4), which announced the excommunication of Archbishop Lefebvre and the four SSPX bishops, Pope John Paul II wrote that the root of Archbishop Lefebvre's 'schismatic act' in carrying out the episcopal ordinations was 'an incomplete and contradictory notion of Tradition. Incomplete because it does not take sufficiently into account the living character of Tradition.'

And so the SSPX is accused of misunderstanding the concept of Tradition and its living character, while the SSPX in turn claims adherence to the 2,000 year teachings of the

Church and accuses the Council of introducing new
teachings contrary to the Catholic Faith which, they say, have
proved disastrous for the Church in the post-Conciliar
period as all the statistics suggest. So naturally this raises the
inevitable question – what is Tradition and what is meant by
the term 'living' in this context?

According to Archbishop Lefebvre in his 1986 *Open Letter
to Confused Catholics*,

> Tradition does not consist of the customs inherited from the
> past and preserved out of loyalty to the past even where there
> are no clear reasons for them. Tradition is defined as *the Deposit
> of Faith transmitted by the Magisterium down through the
> centuries.* This deposit is what has been given to us by
> Revelation; that is to say, the Word of God entrusted to the
> Apostles and transmitted unfailingly by their successors.

As SSPX Bishop Tissier de Mallerais explained in his
discourse *The True Notion of Tradition* given at Versailles
(May 19, 1995), Tradition is immutable just as God is,
because God and the saints who adore Him exist in eternity
which, unlike time, does not change. Thus, new teachings
are not added to the Deposit of Faith, or derived by assimi-
lating elements foreign to it. Instead they are formulated
through progress in precision, as the qualities inherent in a
rough diamond are revealed by the gem-cutter, and through
development in explanation, as the truths contained in the
revealed deposit unfold like a bud which blossoms but
remains, in essence, the same flower.

By this development, truths already contained in the
deposit pass from being implicitly believed to explicitly
stated. Eventually a point which cannot be surpassed is
reached, the point at which truth is defined *ex cathedra* by
a pope, as was the Immaculate Conception by Pope Pius IX,
or the Assumption of the Most Holy Virgin by Pope Pius XII.
Defined truths are therefore irrevocable and no longer
susceptible to development.

Thus the Mass codified by Pope St Pius V in his 1570 bull *Quo Primum*, represents this unsurpassable summit according to Bishop Tissier de Mallerais. The result of centuries of liturgical development, it is the full expression of the dogmas of the Mass. In contrast, the new Mass is a regression rather than a development, since the dogmas are less clearly manifested, the Real Presence less affirmed, the propitiatory sacrifice sidelined and the sacrificing character of the priesthood played down.

Immutable Tradition has an admirable capacity for application to all contingent circumstances, Bishop Tissier de Mallerais also points out. Catholic application involves no change, no mutation of the principles, but instead allows for the development of different applications of the same principles. Tradition is living because it is lived by the faithful, and alive because it applies the eternal and unchanging principles to the problems and necessities of each century. 'But Vatican II let the principles fall, under the pretext of adaptation to the thinking of the modern world,' Bishop Tissier de Mallerais claims.

Therefore Tradition is 'living', is alive, as long as the Deposit of Faith is accurately transmitted. But the new theology adopted by Vatican II has falsified, adulterated and disarmed Tradition, so that sterility and not fecundity is the mark of the Conciliar Church, as evidenced in the dearth of vocations, the widescale abandonment of the Faith, and empty churches.

The Council's professed aim of embracing modern thought and rendering the rites and worship of the Church more suited to the modern age has, according to the SSPX, opened the door to liberalism which denies original sin and insists that human beings are fundamentally good. Accordingly, it is external factors alone which prevent human beings from attaining their fullness, factors identified with the oppressive structures inherent in traditional societies, families and the Church.

Acknowledging no authority other than individual conscience, liberalism insists that traditional and hierarchical institutions warp the human spirit and pervert man's natural tendency to the good. Now that man has at last come of age and realised this, the task in the modern era is to re-fashion the world by dismantling the outdated structures of the past. Since this process involves the vilification of everything traditional, outdated and no longer relevant, the Church before Vatican II is presented as 'out of touch and impotent' wrote Archbishop Lefebvre in *A Bishop Speaks: Writings and Addresses, 1963–1976*. What's more, 'The traditional Church is guilty in her wealth, in her triumphalism; the Council fathers feel guilty at being out of the world rather than of the world. They are already blushing for their episcopal insignia; soon they will be ashamed of their cassocks.'

At the same time, the SSPX sees at work the Modernism condemned by Pope Pius X in his 1907 Encyclical *On the Doctrine of the Modernists*. 'We are now being told that man does not receive truth but constructs it,' claims Archbishop Lefevbre in *An Open Letter to Confused Catholics*. Man constructs truth, say the Modernists, because his desire for the divine originates in his unconscious and manifests itself as a religious feeling which is then converted by the intellect into formulas and dogmas which do not contain the truth but instead are its mere images and symbols.

Believers then come together by sharing their religious experiences and combine to create a society in order to preserve and develop the dogmas they have formulated. In this way the Church is formed as an emanation of the collective unconscious of its members, necessarily limited in expression by time and place and therefore not applicable to all times and places. Continuous change, not homogenous development, is inevitable as the collective unconscious of the faithful continues to manifest itself in the evolution of belief and its symbols.

Interestingly, the modernist architecture adopted by the

Church in recent decades owes its spiritual heritage to Theosophy, a nineteenth-century movement which claimed that the different religions of the world are all necessarily limited manifestations of man's longing for the divine. The aim, therefore, is to pass beyond the restrictions of a particular religion's signs and symbols and attain a true encounter with the one, universal being.

So the participation liturgy promoted by the twentieth-century Liturgical Movement and adopted by Vatican II is most suited to those dismal churches, where the signs and symbols traditionally associated with the Holy Sacrifice of the Mass are notably absent, and the Mass as a memorial meal is celebrated with new ones – pottery chalices, tables for altars, bare brickwork. It is the mystery beneath the symbols that must be encountered through a collectivised liturgy. Statues, rosaries, beautiful high altars – they just get in the way. Original sin, the doctrine of Christ's vicarious satisfaction – they belong to yesterday.

Meanwhile collegiality democratises Church hierarchies and undermines papal authority; the inspirations of the Holy Ghost to an individual bishop are subjected to the vote of the Bishop's Conference; the Church's status as the sole ark of salvation is played down in the name of dialogue. Yes, traditional teaching is found in the Council documents. But the modernist way, so the SSPX argument goes, is to combine truth with error as Pope Pius X pointed out.

Turning to Archbishop Lefebvre again,

> It is because we believe that our whole faith is endangered by the postconciliar reforms and changes that it is our duty to disobey and keep the Tradition ... the greatest service we can render to the Church and to the successor of Peter is to reject the reformed liberal Church. Jesus Christ, Son of God made man, is neither liberal nor reformable.

God bless,
Moyra

A Third Reply to a Confused Catholic

Dear Moyra,

Thank you for your letter on the idea of Tradition – currently one of the points in dispute between the Holy See and the Society of St Pius X. I liked its opening, with the quotation from Bishop Bernard Fellay, very much indeed. The proto-martyr of the Dominican Order is St Peter of Verona who, according to tradition (that word again!), died in just the sort of way the bishop describes. Peter Martyr died writing the Creed with the blood from the wounds received by the assassin's axe. You may notice that, when writing 'tradition', I employed the capital form of the initial letter for the first time I used it, but lower case type for the second. This expresses a distinction which will be crucial to my Third Reply, but meanwhile, may I make one further comment on Bishop Fellay's words?

Without in any way wishing to impugn the admirable zeal they attest, I think it should be said that the martyrs who have watered the field of the Church since the end of the Second Vatican Council have not been, so far as I am aware, members of the SSPX. Rather, they have been ordinary Catholics, whether clergy, Religious, or laity, in such countries as (most recently) Iraq, Algeria, and Somalia. In *Aid to the Church in Need*'s latest report on Christians oppressed for their faith, the Apostolic Administrator of Somalia, Bishop Giorgio Bertin, is reported as saying: 'I do not want to offer my head on a plate too easily. If martyrdom does eventually come, I ask for the strength to go through with it'. That is a rather more likely outcome than that

Bishop Fellay will be pierced with a stiletto on Eurostar by a leader-writer from the London *Tablet*. If readiness to accept martyrdom for the sake of the Faith is a crucial sign of belonging to the Church of Tradition, the honours would appear to be, at best, divided between the Society and the mainstream Catholic body.

What is the principal sign of the Church of Tradition? Raising this question brings me to the main topic of your Letter. Up to a point, I can appreciate Archbishop Levebvre's anxiety that, placed on the wrong lips, Pope John Paul II's phrase 'the living character of Tradition' might be weasel words. What dippings and duckings, shifts and shiftiness, may not be hidden behind that seemingly innocent adjective 'living'? For Blessed John Henry Newman, so we have heard (and heard perhaps rather too often), 'here below, to live is to change'. If so, may not a 'living Tradition' change so much as to transmute into something else, and ultimately change beyond all hope of recognition? 'The kind of person who turned the Last Supper into a Solemn High Mass' are words attributed to Ronald Knox when explaining the elaborateness with which the late Mgr Alfred Gilbey packed an overnight bag. But just as Newman, in describing development, was concerned to show how the Catholic Church, at all points of her history, is self-identical with her first creation at Pentecost (or if you will, on Calvary, when she was constituted in the Mother and Handmaid at the foot of the Cross), so likewise, for Gilbey and Knox, the Supper of the Lord when he instituted the sacrament of his saving Sacrifice, on the one hand, and, on the other, the rites for that sacrament's re-enactment as described in Fortescue and O'Connell or the Sarum Pontifical, put before us *one and the same reality*. What has changed in the Church's life, including her worshipping life, is the presentation of the essence to the milieu, the manifestation of the reality to the circumstances. Not every metamorphosis is a deformation. Indeed, the principal sign of the Church of Tradition is precisely, I would say, that she undergoes metamorphosis without deformation in giving to the world the Revelation bestowed by Jesus Christ and his Spirit on the apostles – a Revelation she presents in ever-changing ways that leave its essence intact.

The difference between 'Tradition' with a capital 'T' and 'tradition' with a lower-case 't' is that the first refers to Revelation as transmitted in the Church's life, while the second refers to the 'ways' in which the Church presents it. The *way* in which the Church presents Tradition may vary in its conceptual idiom, or its liturgical expression, or its artistic style. It can vary in the literary forms it favours, or the spiritualities it uses, or the charisms it deploys. Tradition can be expressed in rigorous ways, as in the 'tradition' of Scholastic theology, or ways that are more relaxed in their attitude to strict canons of evidence and proof, as in the hagiographical 'tradition' that St Peter Martyr died writing the Creed in his blood (the lives of the saints are monuments of Tradition). It is part of the richness of Catholicism – of the 'Catholic tradition' – that it luxuriates in such variety. Not for nothing are we a Church made up of numerous ritual churches, Eastern and Western, with which (I hope) a church of Anglican Catholic tradition will one day be numbered. To limit the Catholic Church to those ways of presenting Tradition typical of a Scholastically-oriented Latin Catholicism in the middle decades of the twentieth century cannot be right. This was Archbishop Lefebvre's mistake.

But to belong to so richly varied a Church – varying in the ways in which it presents Tradition, through time and across space – comes with a price attached. There must be unceasing vigilance to ensure that 'traditions' (lower-case 't') – whether ancient and inherited, or emerging and thus relatively novel – genuinely permit 'Tradition' (upper-case 'T') to make its appearance, really allow Tradition to enter minds and hearts. The tail must not wag the dog, the medium control the message. And this is where Archbishop Lefebvre was exactly right. If Tradition is Revelation itself as transmitted in the Church (and in that sense it may be said to include Scripture, just as in another sense it can be described as complementing Scripture), then the continuance of Christian truth turns crucially on the authenticity of the manner in which this process of transmission is carried out. That is why the Pope and bishops, as, by Christ's will and determination, the chief witnesses to Tradition have a duty to 'guard the deposit'.

Was the deposit guarded at the Second Vatican Council? This will need to be the subject, Moyra, of another exchange. For the moment, it will have to suffice to say that the doctrinal Modernism combated by Pope St Pius X seems to me to play no role at all in the documents of the Second Vatican Council. The place to find it, were it to exist, would undoubtedly be the Council's Dogmatic Constitution on Revelation, *Dei Verbum*. In speaking of how 'the tradition which comes from the apostles develops in the Church with the help of the Holy Spirit', *Dei Verbum* explains such development (para. 8) as 'a growth in the understanding of the realities and the words which have been handed down'. There is here *accretion in understanding* through – we are told – contemplative study (on the model of our Lady at Nazareth) and mystical insight, and this finds sanction in the preaching of those who have received the 'sure gift of truth' (a quotation from the second-century Church Father St Irenaeus) in episcopal consecration. There is no suggestion in this text of *accretion in the deposit itself*. I see nothing here remotely reminiscent of *Pascendi*, no bubbling up from the depths of the collective subconscious, no insinuation that doctrines are only symbols of truth rather than triumphant acquisitions of truth. I find no spirit of accommodation to what Jones, or the man on the Clapham omnibus, can swallow.

That in the situation of anomie in the still not fully resolved crisis in our Church episcopal guardianship has often been lacking, I have no doubt. Nor do I think Neo-Modernism is merely a chimaera. But I am equally convinced that the Church of the post-Conciliar Popes remains the Church of Tradition. What we need now is to recover, for the sake of their great serviceableness, many of the venerable traditions – conceptual, liturgical, and the rest – in which Tradition has been presented. I am speaking of their serviceableness to a Gospel which must, by ever-new inventiveness, be preached to unbelievers in the world of today. This was what was done by the scribe of the Gospels whom the Lord commended for bringing from his treasure-chest things both old and new.

Dear Moyra, I hope there is something helpful in these words.

Yours very sincerely,
Fr Aidan

Fourth Letter from a Confused Catholic: On the Continuity with Tradition of the Second Vatican Council

January 2010

Dear Fr Aidan,

Thank you for your reply to my previous letter on 'The Concept of Tradition', a subject we can't leave behind just yet, since we're shadowing the agenda for the discussions between the SSPX and Rome, and our topic now is – 'The Interpretation of Vatican II in Continuity with Catholic Doctrinal Tradition'.

First of all, though, I wasn't suggesting that the sufferings of the SSPX – ostracisation and exile, not to mention the pain of excommunication – constitute a martyrdom! Neither was I comparing the persecution of Christians across the world with the distress of those who watched the religious life that sustained them being dismantled! It's just sad to think of priests who refused to accept the reforms being driven from their parishes and dying of broken hearts, as Archbishop Lefebvre claims happened in *A Bishop Speaks*.

But were they attached to Tradition or tradition, to a particular tradition of expressing Tradition, to borrow your distinction between 'Revelation as transmitted in the Church's life' and 'the ways in which the Church presents it'? So far, I haven't found any indication in Archbishop Lefebvre's writings of a particular attachment to the liturgical form of the 'middle decades of the twentieth century'. It must have been Tradition with a capital 'T' that concerned him when he wrote in *I Accuse the Council* that,

> the spirit which dominated the Council and which inspired so many of its ambiguous, equivocal and even clearly erroneous texts was not that of the Holy Ghost, but the spirit of the modern world, the spirit of Liberalism, of Teilhard de Chardin, of Modernism, in opposition to the kingdom of Our Lord Jesus Christ.

You say that no Modernist spirit influenced the Council, that there is nothing 'remotely reminiscent of *Pascendi*, no bubbling up from the depths of the collective subconscious, no insinuation that doctrines are only symbols of truth rather than triumphant acquisitions of truth'. And yes, the Council documents do not actually state the Modernist principle that religion is a manifestation of man's unconscious longing for God, or that dogmas are particular expressions of that manifestation, symbolic of the truth but not necessarily true in themselves. But what about the argument that the documents reflect the consequences of these principles?

Tradition is, of course, represented in the Council documents, as it should be. But the issue for the SSPX is the presence, too, of Modernist ideas which have influenced the reforms. So let's look at Pope Pius X's 1907 Encyclical 'On the Doctrine of the Modernists' (*Pascendi*), to see if any of the principles he condemned have found their way into the documents, in spirit if not in letter.

As *Pascendi* (para. 14) states,

> given this doctrine of *experience* united with that of *symbolism*, every religion, even that of paganism, must be held to be true ... On what grounds can Modernists deny the truth of an experience affirmed by a follower of Islam? Will they claim a monopoly of true experiences for Catholics alone? Indeed, Modernists do not deny, but actually maintain, some confusedly, others frankly, that all religions are true.

The question, then, is do you have to believe the underlying principle of unconscious emanations in order to admit its consequence – that all religions are valid paths to the divine? The opinion that each of the world's religions leads to God is readily and repeatedly stated these days, but how many have read *Pascendi*? Can it not be argued that once you accept, or even partly accept, that all religions including Catholicism are true responses to man's unconscious search for the divine, you've accepted a central Modernist tenet, if not the Modernist thinking behind it? You've admitted, or admitted the possibility, that the Church is no longer the one, true ark of Salvation, that Catholicism is just another manifestation of man's unconscious, along with the rest.

Lumen Gentium (para. 8) demonstrates the confusion that can result, according to the SSPX's *SiSi NoNo* series. Combining Tradition with the new, it states,

> This is the sole Church of Christ which in the Creed we profess to be one, holy, catholic and apostolic ... This Church, constituted and organised as a society in the present world, subsists in the Catholic Church ... Nevertheless, many elements of sanctification and of truth are found outside its visible confines.

The above paragraph opens with the traditional doctrine that the Catholic Church is 'the sole Church of Christ'. But then we are told that this sole Church of Christ only 'subsists in the Catholic Church' and that 'many elements of sanctification and truth' are found outside it. Is there not just a hint of a Modernist principle finding its conclusion here?

What's more, the 1965 Declaration on the Relation of the Church to Non-Christian Religions (para. 2) states,

> The Catholic Church rejects nothing of what is true and holy in these religions ... [and] urges her sons to enter with prudence and charity into discussions and collaboration with members of other religions. Let Christians, while witnessing to their own

faith and way of life, acknowledge, preserve and encourage the spiritual and moral truths found among non-Christians, also their social life and culture.

Is it really up to Christians to 'preserve and encourage' the 'spiritual and moral truths' of other religions? And how does this square with the traditional understanding of Christ's call to 'convert all nations'? The Council documents repeatedly urge dialogue with 'men of all opinions' and engagement with the 'ways of thinking and feeling' of the modern age. Thus according to *SiSi NoNo*, 'Vatican II's entire pastoral outlook is polluted because it is founded on *aggiornamento*, that is, on the principle of dialogue with error, rather than with those who are in error in order to convert them.'

To take this argument further, below are quotations from *Pascendi* compared with quotations from the Council documents. For example, *Pascendi* describes how ecclesiastical authority, according to the Modernists, also has its origin in man's religious conscience and is therefore subject to it. For as the Modernists claim, 'To prevent individual consciences from expressing freely and openly the impulses they feel, to hinder criticism from urging forward dogma in the path of its necessary evolution, is not a legitimate use but an abuse of a power given for the public weal.' (para. 25)

Could there be a hint of a conclusion to this principle in the 1964 Decree on Ecumenism (para. 4), 'While preserving unity in the essentials, let everyone in the Church, according to the office entrusted to him, preserve a proper freedom in the various forms of spiritual life and discipline, in the variety of liturgical rites, and even in the theological elaborations of revealed truths'?

Then there's the Modernist claim illustrated in *Pascendi* (para. 26) that, 'evolution in the Church itself is fed by the need of adapting itself to historical conditions and of harmonising itself with existing forms of society.' Now compare this to *Gaudium et Spes* (para. 44),

> The Church has a visible structure, which is a sign of its unity in Christ: as such it can be enriched, and it is being enriched, by the evolution of social life – not as if something were missing in the constitution which Christ gave the Church, but in order to understand this constitution more deeply, express it better, and adapt it more successfully to our times.

Furthermore, *Pascendi* (para. 36) states,

> But while they endeavour ... to prove and plead for the Catholic religion, these new apologists [the Modernists] are more than willing to grant and to recognise that there are in it many things which are repulsive. Nay, they admit openly, and with ill-concealed satisfaction, that they have found that even in its dogma it is not exempt from errors and contradictions.

Which shows signs of a conclusion in the Decree on Ecumenism (para. 6),

> if, in various times and circumstances there have been deficiencies in moral conduct or in Church discipline, or even in the way that Church teaching has been formulated – to be carefully distinguished from the deposit of faith itself – these should be set right at the opportune moment and in the proper way.

It's not difficult to detect a certain mindset coming through in this small sample of quotes from Council documents. This is worrying, because how could any religion withstand the onslaught of Modernism, which sidelines the unique characteristics of disparate traditions and emphasises their similarities, thereby encouraging Catholicism to merge with, and ultimately dissolve into, the world? This impulse can be observed in the modern worship space which has been purged of particular Catholic forms of aesthetic expression, especially those of the 'Scholastically-orientated Latin' tradition you mention. Too often, the liturgy they were designed to accommodate becomes little more than a celebratory display of how modes of worship from different traditions can be combined.

Which leaves one, last question. What's wrong with the Scholastically-orientated Latin Tradition?

Best wishes,

Moyra

A Fourth Reply to a Confused Catholic

Dear Moyra,

Thank you for your new letter, which raises the question of the continuity of the Second Vatican Council with Catholic tradition. I am glad you have accepted my claim that, in and of itself, doctrinal Modernism is not to be found in the documents of the Council. Let me, then, in my turn make the concession to you that Modernism in some sense *is* to be found in those documents (or rather, in some of them and notably in the Pastoral Constitution on the Church in the Modern World). But the sense of Modernism concerned is cultural, *not* dogmatic. What you hold to be hints or innuendos of Modernist attitudes, strangely present in the documents since severed from Modernist doctrines, I would explain as 'cultural Modernism', a term which I now need to define.

By 'cultural Modernism' I mean an optimistic expectation that distinctively modern trends in culture will turn out to be compatible – to say the least – with the truths about humanity held by the Church. What the Church was talking about when she spoke of goodness and truth, freedom and dignity seemed to many to be anticipated, or tacitly taken for granted, by mid-twentieth-century secular sources.

Here are a few of the factors which gave people that impression. There was: the end of the 'hot' phase of the Cold War with its consequent suggestion that ideologically opposed powers could nevertheless agree on the primacy of peace; the success of Christian Democracy in reconstructing Europe after the Second World War in countries like

Germany and Italy; the re-emergence of natural law thinking in international jurisprudence at the trials of the former Nazi leaders; the plausible attempt of philosophers like Maritain to link the budding human rights discourse of the United Nations to the natural law tradition of the Church; the seemingly smooth transition to dignified independence of former colonies equipped with humane constitutions. This list is not exhaustive but it is long enough for my purposes. The combination of these factors helped to create a sense of optimism that world culture and the values cherished by the Church were on an increasingly convergent course. This belief was, I'm sorry to say, the Achilles' heel of the Second Vatican Council.

Not only were a number of these trends purely transient. The way people understood them, or inhabited them in the cultural practices then emerging, was not necessarily compatible with Christianity at all, much less was it favourable to it, and even less could it be described as tacitly anticipating it. Take, for example, freedom as a value. Naturally, the Church of the Council – as the Church before the Council – could agree with humane individuals of all varieties that freedom from the grip of totalitarian regimes is a Good Thing. Building on the optimism of the period, *Gaudium et spes* 54 celebrates a 'new age in human history' in which 'fresh avenues are open for the refinement and diffusion of culture'. But modernity isn't necessarily to be celebrated – not least with regard to how it understands liberty. What of those who, on utilititarian grounds, wanted people to be free from absolute moral laws (the 'Catholic' version of this would shortly be called 'Consequentialism')? What about those who regarded any form of revealed religion as a shackle on intellectual freedom? What of those who held that no society where the Church sets the tone for what beliefs are held and which virtues are cherished can be called a free society? What of those who argued that the historical patrimony of traditional European culture is an incubus on freedom? Or those for whom the promotion of human rights means that every individual should have total autonomy in selecting their own norms for existence – even to the extent of saying a 'faith-education' is child-abuse? I think you get my point! Though the Pastoral Constitution recognizes that freedom may be fostered perversely, as a licence for what is evil, it still paints the concept of freedom with excessively broad brush-strokes. That is so when, without further definition, it remarks that our contemporaries 'make much of this freedom and pursue it eagerly, and rightly so' (para. 17). For we need to know just what, precisely, 'this' freedom is – how people understand what, essentially, 'freedom' *means*. What the Council failed to do was to bring critical intelligence to bear on what was for the most part merely a coincidence in rhetoric between the Western world of the 1950s and 60s and the moral discourse of the Church. If the framers of the Pastoral Constitution had had more respect for Scholastic philosophy they would never have made this mistake.

Moreover: even had the values entertained in civil society beyond the Church coincided in real terms with some of the values fostered by the Church herself, they would still be insufficient to bring human lives in all their inter-relationships to their intended goal. Without sanctifying grace; without faith, hope, and charity; without explicit acknowledgement of the Incarnation and the new order it brings into the world; without a conception of the Holy Trinity as the key to all reality, including social reality; without a conscious orientation to the divine Kingdom adumbrated in the Church and her sacraments, human society – world society – cannot come to its intended goal. Traditionalists often criticize the so-called 'new theology' of the 1940s and 50s, which sought to marry with Scholasticism the teaching of the Church Fathers in an enriched doctrinal synthesis (and in that way, to answer the last question in your Letter, went beyond Scholasticism towards a more holistic grasp of

Tradition). But if the framers of the Pastoral Constitution had had more respect for that theology, associated as it is with the name of the *peritus* (Council 'expert'), Henri de Lubac, SJ, they would not have spoken with two voices on that most crucial of questions. Rightly, de Lubac's theology wants grace *always to lead nature to nature's end*. For specifically New Testament faith, it hardly suffices to say, with the Book of Sirach (15:14), that God has left man 'in the hand of his own counsel', such that he 'can seek his Creator spontaneously, and come freely to utter and blissful perfection through loyalty to him' (*Gaudium et spes* 17, while citing the Sirach text).

What we have to do now, Moyra, is to make sure that the naïve and, consequently, ambiguous statements of the Council fathers on matters of human culture are, for the future, interpreted in the light of their more focused doctrinal references which indicate the vital importance of the natural law and divine Revelation. For the Council texts have valuable things to say not only about the wisdom of God inscribed in the creation but also about grace, Christ, and the Trinity's outreach to us in the Church and the sacramental life, all with a view to our entry into the final Kingdom.

This is, in fact, my chief hope for the present dialogue between the Holy See and the Society of Saint Pius X: namely, that it will produce an 'authentic' – i.e. authoritative – interpretation of the documents where they are, in their general tenor, least satisfactory, which is where they touch on matters of human culture, and that it will do so along something like the lines I am suggesting now.

That will not entail any denial that there are countless instances where actual grace is at work in human lives outside the visible boundaries of the Church. Grace, so understood, is always at work, saving people from the worst consequences of the Fall; nudging them towards genuine, not merely putative, truth, goodness, beauty; preparing them for conversion to the Gospel; neutralizing the efforts of the fallen angels to use man-devised religions, philosophies, institutions, moral codes, for their own destructive ends. There may even be grace-enabled ways in which humanity not only preserves some of the goods with which it was created but is united, anonymously, with God in Christ in his saving work on the Cross and in the Resurrection, and so brought, without awareness of the fact, to evangelical holiness, though of such ways Revelation does not speak. They are, as the Council itself wisely puts it – in the Pastoral Constitution, in fact! (para. 22) – known to God alone.

The confusion engendered by cultural naiveté produced the 'dismantling' of so much of the institutional life of the Church which – as, dear Moyra, you rightly say – so distressed many, undermining the confidence of traditional Catholics in the Council in the later 1960s and since. I think not only of the consequences for preaching and, in some places, the spirit in which the Liturgy was conducted but also of the effective secularisation, in various countries, of so many Catholic universities, hospitals, schools, trade unions, political associations and even Religious congregations and programmes of catechesis. The 'knock-on' effects have been truly horrendous. That is why, this time, we must get this right.

Moyra, thank you for bravely raising these issues, and encouraging me to think them through with you.

Yours in Christ,
Fr Aidan

Fifth Letter from a Confused Catholic: On Ecumenism

January 2010

Dear Fr Aidan,

Thank you for your reply to my last letter. But could I just mention one small point before tackling the subject here which, in line with the agenda being followed between the SSPX and Rome, is, 'The Unity of the Church and Catholic Principles of Ecumenism'. I didn't exactly say that 'doctrinal Modernism is not to be found in the documents of the Council'. While I did acknowledge that the Council documents do not actually state Modernist principles as presented in Pope Pius X's famous Encyclical *Pascendi*, my argument was that the documents do indeed contain ideas which arise from these principles. So the question here is – to what extent are these ideas present in the Council's 1964 *Decree on Ecumenism (Unitatis Redintegratio)*?

Keeping to Ecumenism between the Church and Protestantism in all its forms, there is little difference between the views of the SSPX and those of at least one pre-Conciliar pope. In *An Open Letter to Confused Catholics*, Archbishop Lefebvre describes Ecumenism as 'a tendency especially dangerous to the Faith, the more so because it masquerades as charity ... we cannot unite truth and error so as to form one thing, except by adopting the error and rejecting all or part of the truth. Ecumenism is self-condemnatory.'

Similarly, in his 1928 Encyclical *Mortalium Animos*, Pope Pius XI writes of the budding Ecumenical movement of his time and warns Catholics not to be deceived by 'the outward appearance of good' since 'beneath these enticing words and blandishments lies hid a most grave error'. Given that unity is a mark of the Church, since the Church is ONE, holy, Catholic and Apostolic, the error lies in the claim that unity only existed in apostolic times, to be later replaced by distinct churches and communities divided by differences of opinion which should now be put aside and 'from the remaining doctrines a common form of faith drawn up and proposed for belief'.

Having questioned how unity can be achieved between those who 'retain each his own opinions and private judgement', Pope Pius XI has this to say on Ecumenism:

> the Apostolic See cannot on any terms take part in their assemblies, nor is it anyway lawful for Catholics either to support or to work for such enterprises; for if they do so they will be giving countenance to a false Christianity, quite alien to the one Church of Christ. (para. 8)

Now, everyone says that Vatican II produced no new teachings or defined any new doctrines. But did it introduce new ideas and ways of thinking not defined as doctrines but practically written in stone anyway? Because the *Decree on Ecumenism* states, 'The sacred Council exhorts ... all the Catholic faithful to recognise the signs of the times and to take an active and intelligent part in the work of ecumenism.' (para. 4) And, 'In certain circumstances, such as in prayer services "for unity" and during ecumenical gatherings, it is allowable, indeed desirable that Catholics should join in prayer with their separated brethren.' (para. 8) Far from adhering to a 'false Christianity', Protestants are termed 'separated brethren' by Vatican II.

Furthermore, the *Decree on Ecumenism* contains another new idea, one which Pope Pius XI denounced. Catholic theologians are told that in Ecumenical dialogue, they 'should remember that in Catholic doctrine there exists an order or "hierarchy" of truths, since they vary in their relation to the foundation of the Christian faith.' (para. 11)

Wasn't the 'hierarchy of truths' an idea proposed by the modern theologian Yves Congar? Isn't this what Pope Pius XI warned against when he referred to 'that distinction which some have seen fit to introduce between those articles of faith which are fundamental and those which are not fundamental . . . as if the former are to be accepted by all, while the latter may be left to the free assent of the faithful.' (para. 9)

Because, however you explain it, the term 'hierarchy of truths' will be taken to mean that some truths are more significant than others. The 1970 document *Reflections and Suggestions Concerning Ecumenical Dialogue* (part IV, para. 4b), suggests how this new idea can be understood. 'For example, the dogma of Mary's Immaculate Conception . . . presupposes, before it can be properly grasped in a true life of faith, the dogma of grace to which it is linked and which in its turn necessarily rests upon the redemptive incarnation of the Word.'

But the Dogma that Mary, Mother of God, was conceived without original sin, is a teaching accessible to everyone. Why complicate matters in a pastoral context when, combined with the term 'hierarchy', the result is bound to be that this Dogma will be sidelined in Ecumenical dialogue? Pope Pius XI pointed to the error of putting aside differences in order to achieve a common set of beliefs. Is the Immaculate Conception to be put aside so as not to upset Protestants?

Not according to *Mortalium Animos*, since,

> all who are truly Christ's believe, for example, the Conception of the Mother of God without stain of original sin with the same faith as they believe the mystery of the August Trinity, and the Incarnation of our Lord just as they do the infallible teaching authority of the Roman Pontiff. (para. 9)

If thinking which arises from Modernist principles is indeed present in the *Decree on Ecumenism*, it should reveal itself both in new ideas and in the sidelining of traditional doctrines, since according to Pope Pius X in *Pascendi*, Modernists believe that religion, the Church, tradition and dogma are manifestations of man's unconscious search for the divine and can thus be adapted as man's unconscious determines. Overall, the trend will be towards universality, in which the particular and unique teachings of the Faith are played down in favour of what is common to all.

Not only are new ideas present in the *Decree* – one certain to lead to traditional doctrines being passed over – but past failings of the Church are also alluded to, this being a Modernist strategy to justify change as *Pascendi* points out. For example, 'often enough, men of both sides were to blame' for the separation of communities from the Church. (para. 3) And renewal is necessary because 'in various times and circumstances, there [may] have been deficiencies in moral conduct or in the way that Church teaching has been formulated.' (para. 6)

Of course tradition is present in the *Decree*, as in all Council documents. But what else is present, or not present? Although the *Decree* extols the virtues of the 'separated brethren', it does admit that, among other things, the Protestants 'have not preserved the proper reality of the eucharistic mystery in its fullness'. (para. 22) And the same paragraph continues, 'nevertheless, when they commemorate the Lord's death and resurrection in the Holy Supper, they profess that it signifies life in communion with Christ and await his coming in glory.' The 'doctrine of the Lord's Supper' is then suggested as a suitable subject for Ecumenical dialogue.

However the Holy Sacrifice of the Mass is not considered a subject suitable for Ecumenical dialogue. Protestants might commemorate the Last Supper, but they deny Transubstantiation and don't believe in the necessity of offering the Body and Blood of Christ to God as satisfaction for the sins we daily commit. Has the traditional doctrine that the Mass is a propitiatory sacrifice, which is not even mentioned in the Council's *Constitution on the Sacred Liturgy* as previously argued, also been sidelined to appease Protestants?

Archbishop Lefebvre certainly thought so, and it is one of the SSPX's claims that the reforms have Protestantised the Mass. In *A Bishop Speaks: Writings and Addresses 1963–1976*, Archbishop Lefebvre compares the changes introduced by the Council with the changes introduced by Martin Luther, changes which reflected Luther's view of the Mass as merely a 'sacrifice of praise and thanksgiving, but certainly not an expiating sacrifice renewing and applying the sacrifice of the cross.'

Luther believed that Mass is offered by God to man, not by man to God. He abolished the Offertory and the prayers at the foot of the altar; turned the rite into a Liturgy of the Word followed by Communion; introduced the vernacular; turned the priest round to face the people; introduced tables for altars; and rejected the sacrificing priesthood with the claim that all Christians are priests.

All of which sounds uncomfortably familiar, especially as the *Decree on Ecumenism* actually states, 'Church renewal has notable ecumenical importance ... the biblical and liturgical movements, the preaching of the Word of God and catechetics, the apostolate of the laity ... All these should be considered as promises and guarantees for the future progress of ecumenism.' (para. 6)

So to end, can Catholic principles of Ecumenism mean anything other than proclaiming the teachings of the Church in their fullness and entirety, while praying for and welcoming those who would into the unity which the one, true Church of Christ alone possesses?

Kindest regards,
Moyra

A Fifth Reply to a Confused Catholic

On Inter-Religous Dialogue

Dear Moyra,

Thank you for your epistle on ecumenism, where you ask: are the principles of Catholic ecumenism, as laid down by the Second Vatican Council, consistent with the teaching that the gift of unity promised by Christ to his followers endures in the Catholic Church and in her alone? Actually, you had already mentioned the topic of ecumenism, and the question of inter-religious dialogue, sometimes bracketed with it, in your previous letter, but I wanted to keep my powder dry on both these fronts ...

Before getting into the meat of the new topic, I must address what in this fifth letter you open by calling a 'small point'. Moyra, I have to say that your 'small point' is a very big point indeed! To agree that the documents of the Council do not contain Modernist principles but to assert that nonetheless they include Modernism-derived theses or ideas goes beyond what I understand to be the limits of acceptable criticism *if we are speaking of doctrinal Modernism in the proper sense*. As I've stressed in the course of our exchange, we can legitimately point out failures of prudence on the part of the Council fathers (a latitudinarian approach to liturgical adaptation and an insufficiently critical view of cultural modernity have been my examples here). We may also point out weaknesses or unilateralism in the formulation of the Conciliar teaching (the document on religious liberty – another topic we shall be addressing – is, I believe, the worst offender in that regard). I draw the line, however, at the rejection of the doctrinal intentions embodied in the Council documents *even if those intentions are said to function at the level not of principles but of derived ideas*. I accept that at almost all points the Council does not seek to define doctrine in a single act of infallible interpretation. (The exception, as the late cardinals Yves Congar and Avery Dulles were agreed, is the passage on the divine origin of the episcopate in the Dogmatic Constitution on the Church [*Lumen gentium* 21].) But I think that the Council's other doctrinal theses must be accepted as well. They need to be accepted inasmuch as they are starting-points for the reiterated or everyday ('ordinary') magisterial pronouncements of the post-Conciliar popes (and the wider episcopacy), and inasmuch, too, as they are legitimate developments of what was already found in Tradition as received in the pre-Conciliar Church.

What is *wrong* with Lefebvrism is its claim that the distinctive theses of the Council are *not* legitimate developments of this kind, and that, accordingly, the ordinary magisterium of the Church now finds itself in a condition of internal self-contradiction. That this is an erroneous judgment does not, however, abrogate what is *right* with Lefebvrism which is its critique of the sub-Catholic mind-set the theses in question have been taken to justify by those who use them to forward the agenda of theological liberalism, which itself is liberal Protestantism in thin disguise.

May I now apply all this to the matter in hand? The key doctrinal thesis presented by the Conciliar Decree on Ecumenism is found in the teaching that genuine ecclesial 'elements' are to be found outside the unity – the 'visible boundaries' (*Unitatis redintegratio* 3) – of the Catholic Church, such 'elements' being taken to cover both means of sanctification (appropriating salvation) and doctrinal truths (understanding rightly what such appropriation entails).

Let's take the 'means of sanctification' first. For over fifteen hundred years Catholicism has rejected St Cyprian's view that there can be no sacraments outside the visible unity of the Church. (The Cyprianic view is still, by the way, an influential opinion in Eastern Orthodoxy.) That rejection alone is sufficient to warrant what the Council says about the means of sanctification. When in the late sixteenth century schismatic Oriental bishops in the Ukraine entered into Catholic communion they were recognized as already the sacramental high priests of their communities, true bishops in the apostolic succession. Again (to move from the sublime to the cor blimey), when I was received into the Catholic Church in 1966 I underwent conditional Baptism not because there was any doubt about the sacramental reality of Baptism as conferred in the Church of England but because Anglicans had occasionally departed in practice from the defining norms for that sacrament, norms they accepted in theory. Had I been Orthodox, moreover, I should not have needed to be confirmed.

Now let's take 'doctrinal truths'. The Council of Trent did not feel a need to lecture Lutherans about the Trinity, any more than the Scholastic theologians of all periods felt a need to correct the Greeks about Christology. It is true that some Scholastic theologians so exalted the role of Church authority in the making of the act of faith that no one could (such theologians said) make a properly Christian act of faith unless they accepted the content of the faith specifically from the hands of the Catholic Church. That has never been, however, the official position of our Church. Reunion Councils like Florence always assumed they were dealing with people who were heterodox on one or more heads, not with those who might just as well be in outer darkness. The teaching of Vatican II about the elements of truth and sanctification in non-Catholic Christian bodies (how many elements and of what scope varies, of course, in dependence on which such body we are talking about) is simply a consolidation at the level of doctrine of much that was taken for granted in the preceding tradition.

It follows that while the unity of the Church of Christ endures exclusively in the Catholic Church (*full communion* with the Mystical Body of Christ means, specifically, adherence to the Catholic Church with its Petrine centre), not everything that can be called 'genuinely ecclesial' is included in the visible unity of the Catholic Church so understood. To say that the Mystical Body 'subsists' in the Catholic Church is convenient shorthand for that rather long sentence I've just written.

Does the persistence of these elements of truth and sanctification mean the Catholic Church should send representatives to every possible kind of pan-Christian jamboree? Of course not. Pius XI had good reasons for supposing that the officially organized Protestant (and, to a much lesser extent, Eastern Orthodox) ecumenical movement in the early part of the twentieth century had a marked tendency to doctrinal indifferentism. By the 1950s, however, when the original 'Life and Work' side of the ecumenical movement had been thoroughly integrated with the more recent 'Faith and Order' side, that was no longer the case: professional ecumenists took doctrine very seriously indeed. The early 1960s were a good time to prepare the way for Catholic participation.

By saying so, do I mean that the *de facto* pursuit of ecumenism by Catholics since the Second Vatican Council has been an unreservedly good thing? I mean nothing of the sort. There have been particular irresponsible actions. There has been a widespread unwillingness to raise the question of the unique claims of the Catholic Church. The overall effect has been to lodge in some people's minds a sense that 'all the churches are the same; it doesn't matter, really'. But that is not because the Decree on Ecumenism has been observed. It is because it has been traduced. Imagining the 'hierarchy of truths' means that some truths are less true than others is one example of letting Catholic ecumenism down. Imagining ecumenism means Catholics must become more like Protestants, rather than, say, more like the Orthodox is another.

Of course we are not, in fact, to become 'more like' either. That way of putting it is entirely superficial. We are to bring into the unity of the Church all the riches found in the separated churches and communities on the basis of the 'elements of truth and sanctification' they have preserved – even if not all their members come to join us, though we should dearly like it if they did. In my opinion, authentic Uniatism and true ecumenism come down (or rise up) to the same thing. So you see from this conclusion, dear Moyra, that for once we are in agreement *in the end*.

> Kindest wishes in the Lord,
> Fr Aidan

Sixth Letter from a Confused Catholic: On Inter-Religious Dialogue

February 2010

Dear Fr Aidan,

Thank you for your reply to my letter on Ecumenism in which you maintain that I went beyond 'the limits of acceptable criticism' by asserting that the documents of Vatican II contain 'Modernist-derived theses or ideas'. Since we are now getting to the heart of the matter, perhaps I could respond to this before addressing the next topic on the agenda for discussion between the SSPX and Rome – 'The Relationship Between the Church and Non-Christian Religions'.

You say it is permissible to point out the Council's faults, for example 'failures of prudence' and 'weakness', but that the 'doctrinal intentions embodied in the Council documents' must be accepted 'insofar as they are legitimate developments of what was already found in Tradition as received in the pre-Conciliar Church'. This, then, is surely the crucial point, because if Vatican II's 'doctrinal intentions' do not represent 'legitimate developments' of Tradition, then Catholics have the right to reject them just as the SSPX has done.

'We refuse and have always refused to follow the Rome of the neo-Protestant trend clearly manifested throughout Vatican Council II and, later, in all the reforms born of it,' stated Archbishop Lefebvre in his famous Declaration of 1975. 'The only attitude of fidelity to the Church and to

Catholic doctrine appropriate for our salvation is a categorical refusal to accept this reformation.'

The question must be: do legitimate developments of Tradition include sidelining teachings of the Church and/or introducing new ideas from outside the Deposit of Faith? Because as argued in my second letter, the Council documents have sidelined Traditional doctrine on the propitiatory character of the Sacrifice of the Mass as defined by the Council of Trent. In fact the *Constitution on the Sacred Liturgy* has omitted this teaching altogether and not once, in over fifteen years as a Catholic, have I heard this teaching proclaimed by the conciliar Church.

At the same time, does the new notion presented in the *Decree on Ecumenism* that 'in Catholic doctrine there exists a hierarchy of truths', an idea condemned by Pope Pius XI in his encyclical *Mortalium Animos*, represent legitimate development? And is it not pure innovation to say, as the Council documents do, that a priest is the 'president of the assembly who have gathered to celebrate the Eucharist'?

Because according to Tradition, as Archbishop Lefebvre points out in *A Bishop Speaks*, 'It is the priest who offers the holy sacrifice of the Mass, and the faithful *participate* in this offering, with all their hearts, with all their soul, but it is not they who offer the holy sacrifice of the Mass.' It is the priest alone who acts *in persona Christi* and who, by virtue of the words of consecration which he alone pronounces, makes the Divine Victim truly present on the altar before offering Him as a propitiatory sacrifice to the Father. Can 'president of the assembly' adequately convey the awful dignity of the priest who alone has the power to call down God from heaven and hold Him in his consecrated hands?

However, to do justice to the subject of this letter, let us agree that the Council had faults but pass over the above stumbling blocks in true, ecumenical fashion. At any rate, the Council's 1965 *Declaration on the Relation of the Church to Non-Christian Religions (Nostra Aetate)*, is a short document which opens with a statement to rival *Gaudium et Spes* for the naive optimism you have previously alluded to.

It states, 'In this age of ours, when men are drawing more closely together and the bonds of friendship between different peoples are being strengthened, the Church examines with greater care the relation which she has to non-Christian religions.' And so the scene is set for a rethink of the Church's position, slap-bang in the middle of a century estimated by the United Nations to be the most murderous in history.

The *Declaration* certainly speaks with admiration of the non-Christian religions. For example, it asserts of the Hindus (para. 2) that, 'They seek release from the trials of the present life by ascetical practices, profound meditation and recourse to God in confidence and love.' And of the Muslims (para. 3) that,

> They strive to submit themselves without reserve to the hidden decrees of God, just as Abraham submitted himself to God's plan, to whose faith Moslems eagerly link their own. Although not acknowledging him as God, they venerate Jesus as a prophet, his virgin Mother they also honor, and even at times devoutly invoke.

But which God do the Hindus have recourse to – Vishnu, Krishna, Kali? And I have always thought that the Muslims 'strive to submit themselves without reserve' to Allah. Reading these paragraphs in full gives the distinct impression that the followers of Hinduism and Islam worship the same God as Catholics but in a different form, since the whole drift of the document is to emphasise what the different religions have in common. The fact that Islam does not acknowledge Christ as God is simply glossed over.

'The keynote of the reform is the drive against certainties,' claimed Archbishop Lefebvre in *An Open Letter to Confused Catholics*.

Catholics who have them are branded as misers guarding their treasures, as greedy egotists who should be ashamed of themselves. The important thing is to be open to contrary opinions, to admit diversity, to respect the ideas of freemasons, marxists, muslims, even animists. The mark of a holy life is to join in dialogue with error.

Being judgemental is, in our time, considered the greatest sin of all. Error, and the state of being in error, are concepts which do not sit easily with the contemporary mind. St Cyprian's formula, 'Outside the Church there is no salvation', seems harsh and exclusive in a culture which relentlessly promotes tolerance and inclusivity in order to promote the universal and render the particular insignificant. But the Tradition of the Church recognises three ways of receiving baptism – the baptism of water; the baptism of blood, i.e. that of martyred catechumens; and the baptism of desire. Baptism of desire can be explicit in the case of a catechumen who dies before receiving baptism by water, and it can also be implicit. In *An Open Letter*, Archbishop Lefebvre explains,

> This consists in doing the will of God. God knows all men and He knows that amongst Protestants, Muslims, Buddhists and in the whole of humanity there are men of good will. They receive the grace of baptism without knowing it [and] become part of the Church ... The error consists in thinking they are saved by their religion. They are saved in their religion but not by it.

Therefore the Traditional view of the non-Christian religions follows from the fact that Christ founded only one Church. As Archbishop Lefebvre further explains,

> There is only one Cross by which we are saved, and that Cross has been given to the Catholic Church. It has not been given to others. To His Church, His mystical bride, Christ has given all graces. No grace in the world, no grace in the history of humanity is distributed except though her.

A certain bravery is required to announce this in today's so-called secular society, which neatly brings me to a non-Christian religion not mentioned in the *Declaration*. I say 'so-called' secular society because of course what we see around us isn't secularism, it's Paganism. England in particular and Europe in general, is turning Pagan again, and what is on the cards is some kind of neo-Roman empire in which you can worship any god, or gods, you like as long as you don't claim that yours is the one, true one. And so we have suicide as an honourable act again; the worship of wealth and fame; the cult of the body; and bread and circuses to keep the masses quiet.

Just as Ecumenism tends towards a one-size-fits-all version of Christianity, Modernism aims for a one-size-fits-all religion, or rather spirituality, which offers universal values and a deified image of man, while also accommodating a profusion of local cults, household gods and superstitions which can be called upon for protection and the granting of good fortune.

The demands of Catholic charity should determine the relationship of the Church to non-Christian religions, a charity which cannot include keeping quiet about the truth in its fullness and entirety so as not to upset people. But do the men of the Church still believe they have the truth? Not according to Archbishop Lefebvre in *An Open Letter*:

> They refuse to say – even priests, seminarians and seminary professors – that the Catholic Church is the only Church, that she possesses the truth, that she alone is able to lead men to salvation through Jesus Christ ... They sometimes grant it a slight superiority, if you press them.

How then will you convert the Pagans?

Best wishes,
Moyra

A Sixth Reply to a Confused Catholic

Dear Moyra,

Thank you so much for your Sixth Letter, where you broach the topic of the Second Vatican Council and inter-religious dialogue. You begin, though, by raising again the question of the doctrinal intentions of the Council as expressed in its documents at large. I agree with you that this is the heart of the matter, since what we think about it will determine the spirit in which we approach *all* the Conciliar texts – whether on inter-religious dialogue or on anything else.

We are at one in saying that any Catholic may legitimately call into question the wisdom of the Council's prudential statements – about the reform of worship, say, or the helpfulness or otherwise to the Gospel of contemporary culture. Where we differ is in this: I do not believe we have a similar liberty where the doctrinal statements of the Council are concerned *even if we find these to be in some regard ambiguous in character*. My reason for saying so is straightforward: in evaluating any General Council, legitimately convoked and ratified, an orthodox mind will always take a benign view of the doctrinal intent of the fathers concerned. I take an example from the patristic centuries. A secular historian, or an historian working outside the Great Church, might well wonder whether the fathers of the Council of Chalcedon (451) understood the single person of the Word incarnate to be the pre-existent Word or, rather, a person constituted by the coming together of that Word and the humanity taken from Mary, for there is an ambiguity in the formulation. A Catholic historian will want to defend the intentions of the fathers of Chalcedon, in the light not only of the subsequent clarification of the meaning of the Chalcedonian definition at the Second Council of Constantinople (553) but also of Tradition as a whole. The ground of so wanting is simply the ecumenicity of the Council which implies its preservation from doctrinal error by the guidance of the Holy Spirit.

Before addressing the substance of our main issue in the sixth exchange, might I just look quickly at the three examples you give of defective doctrinal intention as found in particular Conciliar texts? First, the topic of the ends of the Mass – including not only its propitiatory character but its petitionary character more widely – was not raised by the fathers of the Second Vatican Council, but those ends are implicitly acknowledged in the statement of the Constitution on the Liturgy that 'especially through the divine sacrifice of the Eucharist, "the work of our redemption is carried on"' (*Sacrosanctum Concilium* 2). Secondly, you mention the question of the hierarchy of truths. What Pius XI condemned was the drawing of a distinction between fundamental and non-fundamental articles such that the former were mandatory for Christian faith and the latter optional. That the intention of the fathers of Vatican II was not contrary to the pope's judgment is plain from their statement in the Decree on Ecumenism that doctrine must be presented 'in its entirety' (*Unitatis redintegratio* 11) even if some elements within it are more intimately related than are others to the basis of the faith (I take it no sane person could possibly hold that the doctrine of indulgences, say, was equally closely related to that basis as is, for example, the doctrine of the Trinity). Thirdly, you cite the description of the celebrant of the Mass as 'presider'. While, so far as I can see (I may have missed something here), the Conciliar texts use this term only for a bishop-celebrant, it has New Testament justification in St Paul's reference to ordained ministers in the First Letter to the Thessalonians as 'those who preside over you in the Lord' (5:12): words which, in a Catholic or Orthodox perspective, may well be regarded as a Eucharistic allusion. But, again, if we wish to construe aright the intention of the Council fathers in re-appropriating this sort of ancient language we need to bear in mind their statement – as crystalline as anything Archbishop Lefebvre could wish – in the Decree on the Life and Ministry of Priests: 'Through the hands of priests and in the name of the whole Church, the Lord's sacrifice is offered in the Eucharist in an unbloody and sacramental manner until he himself returns'. I have been told that, before the polarization of the post-Conciliar period, Mgr Lefebvre was particularly pleased with this document – and this report is born out by the official biography which was written by his close collaborator, Bernard Tissier de Mallerais, one of the four men he raised, uncanonically, to the episcopal order.

Of course, what has been *done* with these documents, so read, is a totally different matter. The decline of stipendiary Mass-offerings reflects lack of instruction about those ends of the Mass which go beyond the spiritual good of those immediately present. The notion of the hierarchy of truths has been taken to justify a casual attitude towards specifically Catholic doctrines. And as to 'presidency', in its present-day connotations (whatever it may have meant to the apostle) it's difficult to think of any synonym for celebration of the Mass more calculated to insinuate the banal.

So, Moyra, the spirit in which I approach *Nostra aetate*, the 'Declaration on the Relation of the Church to Non-Christian Religions', is not going to be one of looking for bogeys. I hope, however, that the trio of examples I've just given you illustrates the way a benign reading does *not* mean relaxing doctrinal vigilance on the spurious ground that, after 'Vatican II', anything goes.

When we find the document under discussion encouraging Muslims to 'forget the past' in their relation with Christians, it is difficult to deny your opening charge of naïve optimism. That particular passage is not, though, typical of a text which

overall is positive rather than unrealistic. But even positive-
ness, like all emotional tones, can be overdone. I find it surpris-
ing that *Nostra aetate* carries so few references to the history
of religion as a story of error, both metaphysical and moral, and
not simply a story of truth and holiness. One does not need to
be a follower of Karl Barth, for whom all humanly initiated
religious activity – i. e. all religion outside the sphere of the
biblical covenants – is intrinsically idolatrous, to think that a
major feature of the Scriptural witness has somehow disap-
peared from view. I remember my novice-master, the late
Geoffrey Preston, OP, saying, 'Surely Pan led men astray'. The
Acts of the Apostles would lead us to think the same was true of
Diana of the Ephesians. And while we're on the Book of Acts
for which the Church's missionary expansion is *the* sign of the
work of the Holy Spirit between Pentecost and the Parousia,
the early victories of Islam, which effectively wiped out the
Church in large areas of North Africa and Western Asia, can
hardly be anything other than counter-signs of the Kingdom of
God.

Still, such silences in *Nostra aetate* do not invalidate the
doctrinal intention of the fathers of the Council which was to
affirm that, by the criterion of evangelical and Catholic truth,
there *are* elements of truth and holiness not only in Judaism
(something we can take for granted, given the biblically
attested divine origin of the faith of Israel) but in religions
outside the Judaeo-Christian tradition as well. Strangely, the
fathers omit to mention what seems to me the anchor-hold
in Tradition for this statement, and this is the early Apologist
St Justin's notion of the 'seeds of the Word' scattered
through paganism, a notion tacitly accepted by the
consensus of the Church Fathers in their (careful) use of
Greco-Roman philosophy, and highlighted in the Council's
Decree on Missions when it speaks of a 'secret presence of
God' in whatever 'truth and grace are to be found among the
nations' (*Ad Gentes* 9). But actually, if, *de facto*, some aspect
of the teaching or the practice of a non-Christian religion is

in accord with the doctrine of the Church about faith and morals, there is, in any case, no logically available ground for denying the statement the Council fathers made. How could there possibly be?

Where Catholic theologians can differ, though, is in their interpretation of how such congruent aspects of, say, the theistic traditions within Hinduism or the ethics of Gautama, come to be in place. We do not necessarily need to invoke for an explanation divine revelation or even sanctifying grace. It may suffice to say that the mercifully incomplete consequences of the Fall left the powers of human nature sufficiently intact for some appropriation of such 'elements' of truth and goodness to be made. Personally, I would go further, and say that the work of Providence (one might think here of the role of the angelic powers) included these religions within its ambit by the bestowal of graces that steadied the minds and focused the wills of those responsible for the elements of truth and holiness concerned. That, of course, is very far indeed from maintaining that these religions are ordinary means of salvation for those who follow their life-ways – even were we to add that the ultimate foundation of such means of salvation is Christ, the Head of the Church. That is the misconception Marcel Lefebvre was keen to exclude.

You ask me how I would convert pagans? Moyra, when you visited Blackfriars Cambridge, I gave you my answer. It is, in effect, the apologia of the Swiss dogmatician Hans Urs von Balthasar (one of my heroes). My answer to you ran: by showing them how the revelation carried by the Church is the greatest – the most comprehensive and beautiful – truth that can be conceived. On that (very enjoyable, I must say!) occasion, you didn't seem to find my reply persuasive. But I'm afraid I have no other to give. I hope this letter finds you in good heart, despite all the difficulties of the Church today. Meanwhile I am, dear Moyra, most sincerely yours,

Fr Aidan

Seventh Letter from a Confused Catholic: On Religious Liberty

July 2010

Dear Fr Aidan,

Perhaps I could begin this letter on Religious Liberty, the last in the series, by challenging the basis of your argument, which seems to be that the inadequate doctrinal formulations contained in the documents of Vatican II must be tolerated as long as sound doctrine is also found.

In previous letters you acknowledged that the Council documents contain 'failures of prudence' and 'weaknesses or unilateralism in the formulation of conciliar teaching'. Your last letter also stated that while some aspects of Vatican II may be questioned, a similar liberty does not exist regarding the Council's doctrinal statements, 'even if we find these to be in some regard ambiguous in character'.

But would this argument stand up in a court of law, where witnesses are required to give 'the truth, the whole truth and nothing but the truth'? Would *Sacrosanctum Concilium* convince a jury, since as you also acknowledge, this important Council document does not even explicitly state a fundamental, traditional teaching on the sacrificial character of the Mass?

The ambiguous nature of many Council statements has long been criticized by the SSPX. Obviously, ambiguity allows for more than one interpretation, as does the presence of new theology alongside traditional teaching. This raises the question – if the Liberal reformers have embraced the new theology contained in the Council documents and put it into practice, are they really to blame if the results, as witnessed by the banality of the contemporary liturgy, are so dire? Surely the aesthetic expression of the traditional liturgy was shaped by the theology of the Holy Sacrifice of the Mass, just as the conciliar liturgy is shaped by the new theology of the Eucharistic celebration at which the priest presides.

According to the SSPX, Vatican II's new theology is contrary to the tradition of the Church and constitutes a rupture with that tradition. Traditional teaching may be present in the 1965 *Declaration on Religious Liberty* (*Dignitatis Humanae*), as it affirms 'the traditional Catholic teaching on the moral duty of individuals and societies towards the true religion and the one Church of Christ.' (para. 1) But how can individuals and societies exercise this moral duty if they are also asked, by new teaching contained in the same document, to abandon it?

Traditional Catholic social teaching proposes the union of temporal and spiritual powers in a Catholic state, as well as the obligation of such a state to regulate and moderate the public expression of other forms of worship in order to defend its citizens against the diffusion of false doctrines which, in the judgement of the Church, endanger their eternal salvation. Going way beyond the pre-conciliar principle of Religious Tolerance, which in a Catholic state the Church has deemed necessary for the preservation of peace, *Dignitatis Humanae* declares, 'the right to religious freedom is based on the very dignity of the human person [and] ... must be given such recognition in the constitutional order of society as will make it a civil right.' (para. 2)

In tune with the egalitarian spirit of the modern age, *Dignitatis Humanae* grants equal rights to all belief systems by asserting the obligation of the state to ensure that all religious communities are free to 'honour the supreme Godhead with public worship, help their members to practice their religion ... [and] ... not be prevented from

freely demonstrating the special value of their teaching.'
(para. 4) Religious Liberty therefore applies to all religions as
the dignity of man requires and the Church now only claims
her share of it. But how can a state obliged to recognise
Religious Liberty for all religions also exercise its 'moral duty
towards the true religion and the one Church of Christ'?
Surely, by granting equal rights to belief systems which
cannot be true, since only Catholicism is true according to
tradition as *Dignitatis Humanae* affirms, Religious Liberty
grants rights to error and promotes the religious indifferentism of the state.

Vatican II's teaching on human dignity is at the root of this
problem, the SSPX claims, because it plays down the distinction between the dignity man possesses by virtue of his
nature, and that which depends upon his actions and which
can be lost by adherence to error. Man's superior dignity in
relation to other creatures, which belongs to him because
God created him in His image and likeness, lost its sublime
character through original sin which stripped man of this
likeness. Thus it is by sanctifying grace that man is supernat-
urally able to know and love God and to enjoy the Beatific
Vision.

Vatican II, however, adopted the secular Liberal view
which disengages human dignity from Truth, renders it inde-
pendent of the obligation to turn the will towards the Good,
and holds that by exercising his autonomy, which in essence
means autonomy from God, modern man has achieved the
highest form of liberty. Accordingly, the culture of the 'rights
of man' rejects the dogma of Original Sin and man's need of
sanctifying grace, and views man as intrinsically perfect and
self-sufficient.

In *Religious Liberty Questioned*, Archbishop Lefebvre
doubts if the new conciliar teaching can be reconciled with
that of Pope Leo XIII's Encyclical *Immortale Dei* which
states,

If the mind asserts to false opinions, and the will chooses and follows after what is wrong, neither can attain its native fullness, but both must fall from their native dignity into an abyss of corruption. Whatever, therefore is opposed to virtue and truth, may not rightly be brought before the eyes of man, much less sanctioned by the favour and protection of the law.

Not surprisingly, this teaching is at odds with the prevalent mind set of our times, as is the very notion of a Catholic State. And yet it wasn't always so. One of the least recognised tragedies to follow in the wake of Vatican II and its new teachings has been the end of the Catholic States, which gave constitutional recognition and legal protection to the Catholic Church while accepting the private practice of other religions. For example, the 1886 Constitution of Colombia declared Catholicism to be the state religion and granted to the Church a primary role in its affairs at all levels.

Then in 1973, encouraged by the Vatican to conform with *Dignitatis Humanae*, Colombia amended its constitution to state merely that Catholicism is the religion of the great majority of Colombians, while the Church in that country surrendered her right to censor public university texts and ensure the use of the Catechism in schools. What's more, the mission territories ceased to be enclaves where missionaries had greater jurisdiction than the government over schools, health and other services, which were eventually brought under government control.

This astonishing development, in which the Church voluntarily surrendered her privileged status – a status appropriate to the 'true religion and the one Church of Christ' the SSPX argues – was repeated in Spain, Italy and Argentina. In the years immediately following Vatican II, Catholic States across the world amended their constitutions in order to conform with the Council's teaching on Religious Liberty, which absolves the state from its obligation towards the Church and her Divine founder, an obligation which exists because the Reign of Christ the King does not stop at the doors of parliaments and legislatures, whether they deny His Kingship or not.

According to Archbishop Lefebvre in *A Bishop Speaks*:

> They thought that they would attract the world by accepting the ideas of modern man ... who is a liberal, who is a modernist, who is a man who accepts the plurality of religions, who no longer accepts the social kingship of our Lord Jesus Christ. This I have heard twice from the envoys of the Holy See, who told me that the social kingship of our Lord Jesus Christ was no longer possible in our time; that we must accept definitely the pluralism of religions. That is what they told me; that the Encyclical *Quas Primas* which is so beautiful, on the social kingship of our Lord Jesus Christ, which was written by Pope Pius XI, would never be written today. That is what they said to me – the official envoys of the Holy See.

As someone who used to be both in the world and of the world, I have long been astonished at the rosy view of contemporary culture and ideas held by so many men of the Church. In my experience, the modern world hates the Church, it really does, even behind the smiles directed at the overtures of liberal, 'open-minded' Catholics. Because the modern world wants the Church to succumb to its values, to dissolve into it and to disappear, as the last vestiges of Christendom are dismantled and the post-Christian age is gleefully ushered in.

'A complete overthrow of the entire tradition and teaching of the Church has been brought about since the Council by the Council,' Archbishop Lefebvre maintains. It is difficult, then, to argue that this does not apply to Vatican II's *Declaration on Religious Liberty*. And it is equally difficult to see how a Church which carries the legacy of a stripped-down, emptied out faith can withstand a world which desires only its end.

Best wishes,

Moyra

A Seventh Reply to a Confused Catholic

Dear Moyra,

Thank you for this powerfully worded letter on the Second Vatican Council and the responsibility of the State authority to the true religion. This will be our last exchange so I must begin, as you yourself do, by reminding readers of the ground-rules of our debate, as I see it.

First, you rightly report that I do not see any theological difficulty about querying the wisdom of some of the reform provisions made by the Council. Matters that turn on the exercise of practical wisdom in particular sets of circumstances do not involve the 'charism of truth' given to the total episcopate, under and with the pope, by virtue of the high priesthood which, by ordination, is theirs. The equivalent of such 'practical provisions' in earlier Ecumenical Councils chiefly takes the form of canons, many of which are now, rightly, set aside. For example, the First Lateran Council forbade monks from celebrating Mass in public churches and from hearing confessions; the Fourth Lateran Council insisted on Jews wearing distinctive dress; the Second Council of Lyons required papal conclaves to be held in whatever city a pope happened to die. And I cannot forbear from mentioning that the Council of Vienne penalized abbots and priors who wore unlaced boots or rode horses with decorated saddles! Under the same heading of 'possible failures in practical wisdom' I would include the misjudgments about contemporary trends I discussed in the Fourth Reply.

Secondly, I have conceded that the doctrinal statements of

a Council (which, obviously, are far more important for the Church of all ages) may be less than balanced or comprehensive in character and thus, by implication, need supplementation, whether from another Council or from other sources. The development of Christological doctrine in the early centuries, from Ephesus to the Third Council of Constantinople, substantiates, I believe, this view. Were the Church to have drawn a line under that development at any point before the last of the four Councils concerned, we should not have had the beautiful equilibrium of our doctrine of the Word incarnate, a pre-existing divine Person now energizing in his two natures, with his twofold divine and human will.

And then thirdly, you note that, for me, a conciliar formulation of Catholic truth may be, in some respect, ambiguous in character. One obvious example at the Second Vatican Council is the teaching on the inerrancy of Scripture in the 'Dogmatic Constitution on Revelation' (*Dei Verbum* 11) which (according, at least, to many interpreters) leaves open two possibilities: that all Scripture is materially inerrant, and that all Scripture is inerrant in the formal perspective of its bearing on human salvation. You ask whether a Council that has produced such ambiguities can still be credited. I reply that, if it cannot, then no more can earlier Councils, the texts of which, at certain points, exhibit grey areas to which the subsequent magisterium, assisted by the theological schools, must attend. Thus, for instance, it is disputed whether the Council of Trent taught that revealed truth is to be found partly in Scripture and partly in Tradition, or, alternatively, that revelation is transmitted wholly in both.

We must not ask for perfection from Councils, even in their strictly doctrinal aspect. It is enough to know that, read according to a hermeneutic of continuity, they will not lead us astray. An Ecumenical Council will never formally commit the Church to doctrinal error. It is, moreover, unfair to ask of Councils what they have not claimed to provide: to demand, for instance, from the Second Vatican Council a doctrinal overview of the Mass considered as Eucharistic Sacrifice, something the fathers of that Council never attempted. I think the 'court of law' to which you appeal would vindicate me on that point, at any rate if equity were among its principles.

Will this, then, be my defence of Vatican II on the neuralgic issue to which we are devoting the bulk of this last exchange of letters, the 'Declaration on Religious Freedom'? In theory it could be, since, while acknowledging the duty of civil society to recognize the Gospel of God, the Council *takes it as read* and proceeds to put forward a further teaching – on the right of persons not to be coerced by the State in their religious convictions – which is *relevant to that acknowledgement but also distinct from it.* The Council did not set itself the task of expounding what it called 'the traditional Catholic teaching'. Where Liberal Catholics have gone astray is in their supposition that the innovatory teaching on the right to religious freedom contradicts the earlier teaching of the Church on the rights of revelation in a Catholic State (thus briefly acknowledged in *Dignitatis humanae* 1). That has proved an extremely damaging mistake.

Not only has it led mainstream Catholics, even when historically and currently the majority in certain societies, more or less to privatize their faith, dismantling the canopy it provides for life together as a whole. It has also become a precedent – or, rather, a pseudo-precedent – for appeals for the deconstruction of other stably possessed doctrines of the Church, notably in family ethics, but by no means exclusively there (the topic of the ordination of women comes to mind). In the words you quote from its opening paragraph (and I have to congratulate you, Moyra, on noticing them, which is more than some people have done), the bishops at Vatican II assert that they propose to leave conceptually untouched the traditional doctrine about a Christian society. What they do instead, in the course of the document, is further to develop the long-standing theology of Christian initiation for which the act of faith may never be forced on anyone, in any circumstances whatsoever. Metaphysically considered, that respect for conscientious lack of conviction turns on the dignity of the human hypostasis (the basic human self), for, *pace* Mgr Lefebvre, the dignity of persons remains intact after the Fall, in line with the doctrine of the Council of Trent that the imagehood of God in man is damaged by original sin, but not destroyed by it. That is the real basis of the 'new' doctrine which, consequently, can claim the status of a homogeneous, not heterogeneous, doctrinal development.

However, unlike (I would say), the Eucharistic doctrine of the 'Constitution on the Liturgy', the 'Declaration on Religious Freedom' occasions a genuine difficulty for orthodox Catholics. As you point out, it is not immediately apparent how to reconcile its acknowledgement of the traditional teaching about the Christendom State with its development of the teaching about the freedom of the act of faith. If we are unpersuaded of a difficulty here, we have only to look at its aftermath. Except among two groups, the period since the Second Vatican Council has witnessed a withdrawal from 'theo-politics' on the part of the hierarchy. Traditionalists and Liberation theologians, neither group popular with Rome, are the two constituencies that have most vocally supported a continuing appeal to civil society to recognize evangelical and Catholic truth not just in the private lives of individual citizens but also in its public institutions, which include, of course, society's own legal form, the State. Does the Declaration bear some responsibility for this dereliction of duty? I do not think we can wholly exculpate the fathers of the Council who were aware of the difficulty involved yet chose (through, I take it, a desire not to prolong further a contentious debate) to restrict to a passing mention their acknowledgement of what I prefer to call, more in the idiom of Chesterton and Christopher

Dawson than Lefevbrists or Liberationists, the thesis of 'Christendom'.

It is true that the State establishment of the Church has produced, historically speaking, many inconveniences. When, during the Third French Republic, anti-clerical polit-icians rejected the Liberal thesis of a 'free Church in a free State' in favour of continuing establishment, they did so because, in the words of one of their number, the maxim could only mean 'an anarchic Church in an impotent State'. A State Church may well enable infidel Statesmen to control the Church, as when ten free-thinkers on the Conseil d'Etat sat around a green carpet choosing bishops. Believing and even devout Catholic politicians and princes have, in the past, demanded their pound of flesh, as the examples of Gallicanism in France and Josephinism in Austria indicate. The secularization of Catholic States has not been without its advantages for the Petrine office-holder.

Nevertheless, I strongly agree with you that publicly recog-nising divine revelation is an entailment of the Kingship of Christ on which, despite its difficulties in a post-Enlightenment society, we must not renege. Where the ethos of society is such that an elected legislature may be trusted to regard the Judaeo-Christian tradition as normative, the Church *should* be accorded her rightful place as 'mother and mistress'. (The Edwardian priest-novelist Robert Hugh Benson's *The Dawn of All* will give you the idea.) Where that is not possible there should at least be, in the former Christendom, a recognition of the historic role of the faith in forming the human patrimony and thus what a bishop of the Church of England, arguing, in the pages of the *Times Literary Supplement,* against disestablishment, has recently termed a 'symbolic privileged position'.

The reason, of course, is not to give ecclesiastics airs and graces. As you, Moyra, with your street-wise sense of realities, recognize, the point is to permeate society and culture to the degree possible with the Christian spirit, and to maximize the number of occasions in civic life where testimony to Christ and his Church might be given. Can this be compatible with acknowledging – under some more generous rubric than tolerance with a view to public order – a place under the sacred canopy of a Christendom society for followers of other religions and none? Our last round of letters throws some light on this. Meanwhile, I hope that the dialogue between the Holy See and the Society of St Pius X will come up with a truly excellent statement on this whole topic – not only for the sake of reconciliation with a minority but to renew the Christendom aspiration of the whole Church. Dear Moyra, if I may say so without offence, you may have been among the particles of grit to produce the pearl in the oyster.

Yours with every best wish for the future,

Fr Aidan

One Last Letter from
a Confused Catholic

August 2010

Dear Fr Aidan,

Now we have come to the end of the debate, but perhaps not quite the end of the discussion, since I've taken the liberty of writing this last letter to you, in the hope that the generosity with which you have responded to my questions so far has not been exhausted. Of course I'm tempted to prolong our correspondence for just a little while longer. But this letter was also prompted by a recent news story which, I thought, seemed to highlight the question of human dignity in the modern age.

The story concerned a particularly newsworthy prison inmate and his intention to sue the authorities for compensation on the grounds that they had failed to protect him from an assault by a fellow prisoner. What attracted my attention, however, was the accompanying legal claim that the human rights of the individual concerned were not affected by his being a convicted double murderer, that he had the same human rights as everyone else. Because what this assertion illustrates, surely, is the very modern view that human dignity remains unaffected by an individual's actions, and that the 'human rights' which arise from this dignity cannot therefore be challenged.

Of course the prison authorities are obliged to protect those in their charge, especially given the existence of a long-standing prison culture which justifies physical attacks

on certain categories of inmates. But does the claim of unassailable human rights contribute to the argument that so
frequently arises elsewhere in the criminal justice system,
creating a tension between those who promote the human
rights of the offender and those who demand justice for the
victim, a tension highlighted by media comment which
regularly polarises along these lines? And is this tension also
evident in society at large, as human rights legislation is
increasingly employed to defend claims against institutions
and 'my rights' advocates are accused of ignoring responsi-
bilities and obligations to others?

Because the Traditional teaching of the Church asserts
that human dignity can indeed be lost. As quoted earlier,
Pope Leo XIII's Encyclical of 1885, *Immortale Dei* (para. 32),
points out, 'If the mind assents to false opinions, and the will
chooses to follow after what is wrong, neither can attain its
native fullness, but both must fall from their native dignity
into an abyss of corruption.' And similarly, in an Intervention
made during the Second Vatican Council and quoted in
Religious Liberty Questioned, Archbishop Lefebvre
observes, 'so long as he clings to error, the human person
falls short of his dignity.'

A fundamental claim of the Society of Saint Pius X is that
the Council's *Declaration on Religious Liberty* has moved
significantly towards a modern view of human dignity, as
demonstrated in statements like (para. 2), 'the right to
religious freedom has its foundation in the very dignity of
the human person.' As already mentioned in my previous
letter, *Dignitatis Humanae* does not fully explain Church
teaching on this important subject, omitting the distinction
between man's 'ontological' dignity which arises from his
essential being, and his 'operative' dignity which depends
upon his actions. In previous letters, however, you have
defended the Council against the charge that its documents
fall short of presenting Traditional doctrines in their entirety.

Meanwhile, in your letter on Religious Liberty you explain

that 'respect for conscientious lack of conviction turns on the dignity of the human' and that 'the dignity of persons remains intact after the Fall, in line with the doctrine of the Council of Trent that the imagehood of God in man is damaged by original sin, but not destroyed by it.' But what is the effect of this damage? According to Tradition, it is to leave man's nature with a wound that not even the grace of Baptism can fully heal, since although the stain of original sin is cleansed by Baptism, the wound remains.

Religious Liberty, according to its opponents, derives from the Liberal concept of an unassailable human dignity and accommodates modern man's refusal to accept that he is Fallen. It is from the dignity he possesses as a human being that the modern Liberal derives his autonomy, the primacy of his conscience, and his full rights. Traditional doctrine is unacceptable to Liberalism because it teaches that the Fall has left man's nature wounded and his intellect darkened, as so much of the evidence around us unfortunately suggests. According to the contemporary view, if human beings fail to meet the ideal, this cannot be due to any fault in man's nature, but must be attributed to external factors which repress, constrict and deny man's true humanity the opportunity to flower in its fullness.

The question of Religious Liberty and the Liberal concept of human dignity on which it rests, is central to the SSPX argument because from this reorientation it cannot help but follow that the doctrines of Christ's Vicarious Satisfaction, the Holy Sacrifice of the Mass, the sacrificing character of the Priesthood, and man's inability to achieve the Beatific Vision without Sanctifying grace, have been sidelined. Assured of his dignity, modern man has no need of propitiation, of sacrifice, or of making satisfaction to God.

Today the preferred message is that Jesus loves us, we're all basically good despite messing up from time to time, and we're all going to Heaven. And even if the claim were to be accepted that an adjustment was required to rebalance the pre-conciliar emphasis on propitiation and supplication more towards one of participation and celebration, it would be difficult to see the result of these moves as anything less than a significant change of direction.

According to Archbishop Lefebvre in *Religious Liberty Questioned*,

> The new thesis on religious liberty bases liberty of action (not to be restrained) in religious matters on the ontological dignity of the person. It is an error: the ontological dignity of man refers only to his free will and not at all to moral liberty or liberty of action. Actually, moral liberty and liberty of action are in relation to the operations or actions of a person and not to his essential being. They have therefore as a foundation the operative dignity of man, or what amounts to the same thing, truth: that is, the actual adherence of the person to the truth. When, on the contrary, man cleaves to error or moral evil, he loses his operative dignity, which therefore cannot be the basis of anything at all.

Sadly, the Catholic States are no more. Forty years on from *Dignitatis Humanae*, and having relinquished her privileged status in those States, the Church is now in a better position to assess the results. Has the promise of 'A Free Church in a Free State' come true? Or has the reality turned out to mean 'A Demoted and Marginalized Church in a State Let Loose'?

Commenting on the concerted efforts of the nations to dismantle the last remnants of Christendom, Bishop Tissier de Mallerais wrote in *Fideliter*, March-April 2005, 'We observe that the conciliar Church cooperates in this work.' Can the break-up of Catholic institutions and the breakdown of Catholic social life, really be attributed solely to the over-enthusiastic and misguided reforming zeal which took hold in the wake of Vatican II? If the autonomous human individual, possessed of a dignity that cannot be diminished and from which his rights are derived, has indeed become the model citizen of the modern age, can adapting the teachings of the Church to this world view achieve anything other than the furthering of its goals? At any rate, the Social Reign of Christ is rarely spoken of these days.

One further matter. As you point out, the act of faith may never be forced upon anyone and that is right, of course. Tradition certainly agrees with this, as confirmed in *Immortale Dei* (para. 36), 'no one shall be forced to embrace the Catholic faith against his will, for, as St Augustine wisely reminds us, "Man cannot believe otherwise than of his own will."'

Admittedly, Religious Liberty sounds more in tune with the freedom-loving spirit of the age than does Religious Tolerance which, in a Catholic State, accepts the practice of other religions but insists on the special status of the one, true, Faith. Why this assertion should not be made is beyond me. It may be anathema to the secular, Liberal view which undermines all traditional belief systems in order to replace them with its own, but surely that is beside the point. At any rate, the age of Christendom is surely over, at least for now, the nations are reverting to Paganism and the Church now finds herself in a situation that the early Christians might recognise. How did they react to the demand that they make offerings to the gods of the Empire?

In a climate of dialogue, the SSPX continues to proclaim the Social Reign of Christ and to insist that Christ's Reign does not stop at the doors of the parliament building or the steps of the town hall. After all, Christ is King, is He not.

Christus vincit, Christus regnat, Christus imperat.

Best wishes,
Moyra

A Final but Not Necessarily Conclusive Reply

Dear Moyra,

We agreed that we should each write a Conclusion to this 'Dialogue with Catholic Traditionalism', and you have chosen to make yours a renewed plea for the Traditionalist concept of human dignity, and the limitations that hedge round that dignity after the Fall of Man. You have settled on this point because you take it to be (if I understand you) the key to all Mgr Lefebvre's criticisms of the Second Vatican Council, its 'letter' as well as its 'spirit'. For if human dignity cannot be lost, and the rights it confers remain enduringly intact, where, one might ask, does this leave the radical need for salvation which has always been the foundation of the Church's claims? If, in some quite fundamental sense, humanity is 'all right', then what is the requirement for a Redeemer? How can we continue to commend the role of the Catholic Church as Mother and Mistress of the nations? Why must the Mass, her central act of worship, be a Sacrifice of supplication and propitiation for miserable offenders, rather than, in all simplicity, an act of praise and thanksgiving for benefits received?

Let me begin by saying I have no difficulty with Archbishop Lefebvre's distinction between 'ontological' and 'operative' dignity as such. To my mind, that distinction points precisely to a dignity that can never be lost, since in one of its modes dignity follows from the very *being* – the 'ontology' – of the human person herself. The tragedy of sin is that we betray that dignity. We are princes who drag our noble robes through muck. Our inherent nobility as images of God doesn't reduce the opprobrium we deserve when we make the Fall our own. On the contrary, that nobility increases our guiltiness. It renders monstrous the evil we do. There is no shred of dignity at work in sinful deeds, no 'operative' dignity to be found there at all. Rather do we demean our high calling – I mean, just as human beings, I am not yet talking of our supernatural vocation – in a way no mere animal could ever do. I am reminded of a former prior of Blackfriars Cambridge, Father Thomas Gilby, who, rather in the spirit of the mediaeval bestiaries, used to remind the congregation here, 'Kingfishers are beautiful birds. But they foul their nests'.

So humanity is definitely *not* 'all right'. It needs what the theologians call *gratia sanans*, the 'healing grace' of the God-Man. It needs the wisdom by which Holy Mother Church can interpret the natural law, the law of creation. It needs the Fountain of mercy that stays ever open in the Sacrifice of the altar. And what humanity is offered by Christ and the Church goes beyond even that. His grace is *gratia elevans*, our movement into the life of God; it is intended as divinization, *theosis*. The Church's Eucharist brings not only graces of repentance and conversion, it also brings about, for those who cooperate fully with the mystery, intimate hidden union with God.

I have no objection, Moyra, to your robust doctrine of sin. After the Fall, the phrase 'human depravity' is not too strong, and what it denotes comes, as you say, from the weakness of the will in its pursuit of the good and the darkening of the human mind as the orientation towards truth falters. Those negative factors can reach the point when, in a well-ordered society, the civil authority will intervene to inhibit the action of the religiously committed individual – despite the 'onto-logical' dignity of the person – as *Dignitatis humanae* itself somewhat laconically observes (para. 2). The Council scarcely expects civil society to follow up the 'Declaration on

Religious Liberty' by accepting 'Thuggee': the ritualised murder, as an offering to the goddess Kali, which recurs from time to time in rural India even today. Likewise, for any crim-inally recognised breach of the moral law, whatever its moti-vation, there is, in a properly functioning society, a price to be paid. If due self-determination implies a right to choose, within reasonable limits, how, where, and with whom one will spend one's life, then a term of imprisonment is, surely, an infringement of human rights – and, where good law is well administered, a praiseworthy infringement at that.

The trouble with the language of 'rights' is it is a wax nose one can press into any shape one likes. As I read recent Church history, the new prominence of rights discourse in the public speech of hierarchs is the work not so much of the Council as of the post-Conciliar popes. In Britain today we have good reason to know it can be both an incubus and a help. At stake in the matter of abortion, is there a woman's right to choose what to do with the reproductive capacity of her own body? Or is that a pseudo-right, the genuine right being the right to life of the infant she conceived? And in any case, where will the mushrooming of asserted rights end, devaluing as it does the very word on whose moral capital it depends? But before we move to eliminate it from our vocab-ulary we need to understand what a pope like John Paul II thought he was doing when he adopted rights language so vociferously. He was attacking in the East the Communist system whose philosophy of dialectical materialism had no room for 'human nature' and thus for 'natural rights'. And similarly he was attacking in the West the legal positivism for which a human right is merely what this or that national legislature happens to say it is. Neither of those errors is compatible with the anthropology of the Church. Natural human rights, when correctly identified, tell us what is justly due to the image of God in man.

Some critics of Traditionalism will say that Mgr Lefebvre's systematic hostility to the language of rights merely places him as a particular kind of Frenchman for whom any mention of the 'rights of man and the citizen' summons up the spectre of the despised Revolution of 1789. As is well known, the Archbishop considered the Council to be the arrival of the French Revolution in the sphere of the Church, the abomination of desolation set up, blasphemously, in the midst of the holy place. No one who is not French can fully understand, perhaps, the power of the counter-revolutionary tradition – the heroic resistance of the Vendée to a godless regime, the hopes placed on the Restoration of the monarchy in 1815, the seizing of the opportunity, at Vichy in 1940, to replace the hated 'Liberty, Equality, Fraternity' of the Republic with a new motto more in keeping with Catholic sensibility: 'Family, Fatherland, Work'. I note that Bishop Tissier de Mallerais, the Archbishop's biographer, is, in his own words, the grandson of a 'disciple and companion' of Charles Maurras, the chief philosopher of the radical Right in France, condemned by Pius XI but contumaciously followed by a number of Catholics (including the said grandfather) until his (partial) rehabilitation by Pius XII. That is not necessarily a criticism of Traditionalism (after all, most of those who attend the churches and chapels of the Society of St Pius X are not even French), but it is nonetheless a fact. Before we rush to judgment on its basis, we should reflect that England has never known a revolution of a comparable order. Though we once killed a king in favour of (eventually) a 'Lord Protector' and replaced an Anglican settlement with first a Presbyterian and then a Congregationalist one, we soon came to our senses (in 1660). So long as we retain our monarchy and the established Church, our *ancien régime* continues, at any rate as a legal form and, however weakened, a cultural force.

We can surely recognize the way the French Revolution – which, not without cause, historians often call 'The Great Revolution of the West', for its influence spread far beyond France – was profoundly subversive of historic Christendom. Writing as an apologist for both the Church and modern

France, Hilaire Belloc sought to defend the Revolution as naturally Christian in spirit and only anti-Catholic by accident. I tend to agree with the English historian of culture Christopher Dawson: its hostility to the Church was fundamental. The Revolution embodied, wrote Dawson, a religion of human salvation. And he went on to add, in words which, no doubt, Mgr Lefebvre could echo: the Tree of Liberty replaced the Cross, the Reason of Man substituted for the Grace of God, and the Revolution itself took the place of Redemption.

I think contemporary Churchmen have made a great mistake whenever they have sought to dismantle what the Anglo-Catholic theologian John Milbank calls the 'remnants of Christendom'. In the Great Commission at the end of St Matthew's Gospel, our Lord asked his apostles to convert *the nations*, and that cannot be done by targeting individuals on an Alpha Course or even the Rite of the Christian Initiation of Adults. It assumes the steady drip, drip, drip, of the water of Revelation throughout culture in a society where custom and education, art and literature, thought and the laws in vigour, insinuate the faith at all levels. I explain that in my attempted manifesto of plenary Catholicism *Christendom Awake*, and seek to apply it to our situation at home in a little book called *The Realm*.

Although what some authors are now calling 'Theopolitics' renders me (in appropriate circumstances) sympathetic to the Traditionalist view of the Catholic State (though the Christendom society is far more than its State form), the primary consideration is not, however, the public law of the Church. It is the proper description of the Church in her continuous, self-identical, believing and worshipping existence. That is why I cannot, Moyra, say to Traditionalists, come and join forces with us (orthodox official Catholics) at any price you may set. The price of rejecting the Council en bloc is too high for me to pay. And indeed we can hardly hope to persuade representatives of the civil order of the merits of Catholic truth if at the same time we call into question the coherence of that truth – the internal coherence of the pre- and post-Conciliar tradition considered as a unity.

The weaknesses I have conceded in the Conciliar documents do not, I believe, outweigh their strengths. True, an occasional text is so bland as to be almost nugatory (*Inter mirifica*, the 'Decree on the Instruments of Social Communication', comes to mind), and set a sad fashion for bureaucratese in Pastoral Letters. Nonetheless, the accents of the great doctors are audible in much that is non-controversial in this corpus of teaching while what *is* controversial (between official Catholics and Traditionalists, I mean) is also of importance. It is important, I hold, for meeting the trio of imperatives which, so I suggested in my 'Introduction' to *The Council in Question*, lay behind Pope John's initiative from the beginning. Encouraging the Church to speak more powerfully to the contemporary world; hastening the reunion of separated Christians; recovering more fully the riches of the ancient tradition: these remain legitimate objectives however inept the ways in which some people – many people, alas – have sought to attain them or further them.

This is the tragedy of the post-Conciliar era, that an instrument of Catholic renaissance has been made into a stone of stumbling. But we believe in the divine ability to bring Easter out of Good Friday. The passion of the Church we have lived through, and still experience, must be for some saving good.

Until we meet again, Moyra,
I am yours very sincerely,
Fr Aidan